THE POWER OF MEMORIES

THE POWER OF POWER MEMORIES

How to Use Them

to Improve Your

Health and Well-Being

FRANK MINIRTH, M.D.

JANET THOMA BOOK

THOMAS NELSON PUBLISHERS

Nashville • Atlanta • London • Vancouver

Copyright © 1995 by Dr. Frank Minirth

Published in Nashville, Tennessee, by Thomas Nelson, Inc., Publishers, and distributed in Canada by Word Communications, Ltd., Richmond, British Columbia.

The Bible version used in this publication is THE NEW KING JAMES VERSION. Copyright © 1979, 1980, 1982, Thomas Nelson, Inc., Publishers.

Library of Congress Cataloging-in-Publication Data
Minirth, Frank B.
    The power of memories / Frank Minirth.
        p.   cm. — (Minirth Meier New Life series)
    ISBN 0-8407-7641-1 (hardcover) :
    1. Memory. 2. Recollection (Psychology) 3. Recollection (Psychology)—Case studies. I. Title. II. Series.
BF371.M55 1995
153.1'2—dc 20   94-30438
                                                          CIP

Printed in the United States of America.
1 2 3 4 5 6 — 00 99 98 97 96 95

The Anger Workbook
   Dr. Les Carter,
   Dr. Frank Minirth
Don't Let the Jerks Get the Best of You
   Dr. Paul Meier
The Father Book
   Dr. Frank Minirth,
   Dr. Brian Newman,
   Dr. Paul Warren
The Headache Book
   Dr. Frank Minirth
Hope for the Perfectionist
   Dr. David Stoop
Imperative People
   Dr. Les Carter
Kids Who Carry Our Pain
   Dr. Robert Hemfelt,
   Dr. Paul Warren
The Lies We Believe
   Dr. Chris Thurman
*Love Hunger: Recovery for Food
   Addiction*
   Dr. Frank Minirth,
   Dr. Paul Meier,
   Dr. Robert Hemfelt,
   Dr. Sharon Sneed
Love Hunger Action Plan
   Dr. Sharon Sneed
*The Love Hunger Weight-Loss
   Workbook*
   Dr. Frank Minirth,
   Dr. Paul Meier,
   Dr. Robert Hemfelt,
   Dr. Sharon Sneed
Love Is a Choice
   Dr. Robert Hemfelt,
   Dr. Frank Minirth,
   Dr. Paul Meier

Love Is a Choice Workbook
   Dr. Robert Hemfelt,
   Dr. Frank Minirth,
   Dr. Paul Meier,
   Dr. Deborah Newman,
   Dr. Brian Newman

Passages of Marriage Series
New Love
Realistic Love
Steadfast Love
Renewing Love
Transcendent Love
   Dr. Frank and Mary
   Alice Minirth, Drs. Brian
   and Deborah Newman,
   Dr. Robert and Susan
   Hemfelt

Passages of Marriage Study Guide Series
New Love
Realistic Love
Steadfast Love
Renewing Love
Transcendent Love
   Dr. Frank and Mary
   Alice Minirth, Drs. Brian
   and Deborah Newman,
   Dr. Robert and Susan
   Hemfelt

The Thin Disguise
   Pam Vredevelt, Dr. Deborah
   Newman, Harry Beverly,
   Dr. Frank Minirth
The Things That Go Bump in the Night
   Dr. Paul Warren,
   Dr. Frank Minirth
The Truths We Must Believe
   Dr. Chris Thurman

For general information about Minirth Meier New Life Clinic branch offices, counseling services, educational resources, and hospital programs, call toll free 1-800-NEW-LIFE.

Contents

Part One: When Memory Works for Us

1. The Power of Our Memories   3
2. Our Mind's Amazing Power to Remember   13
3. The Changing World Inside Our Memories   29
4. Memories—A Mirror of Who We Are   45

Part Two: When Memory Works Against Us

5. Can Our Memories Be Distorted?   69
6. Unhappy Memories—All of Us Have Some   81
7. Preparing to Mend Memories   105
8. Healing Unhappy Memories   121
9. When Memories Will Not Heal   145

Part Three: When Children Remember

10. Shaping Young Kids' Memories   157
11. Shaping Teen Memories   181
12. Meeting a Child's Special Memory Needs   199

Part Four: When Memories Build the Future

13. Building Good Family Memories   213
14. Blessed Memories   235

WHEN MEMORY WORKS FOR US

1

The Power of Our Memories

Elaine Houser's problems scared her already, and they were getting worse. She couldn't sleep well at night, and the constant fatigue and rest deprivation were beginning to affect her work. Her doctor brushed off her complaint with a terse, "You worry too much, Elaine," and prescribed a sleeping pill. She didn't want to take sleeping pills. She wanted to get to the bottom of her health problem and she couldn't.

Her mother was obese until Alzheimer's took over, and she literally forgot to eat. At age thirty-five Elaine was starting down the same road of weight gain, and she dreaded to think what she would look like in a few years.

Elaine herself had memory problems. She was starting to experience annoying, recurring short-term memory losses. She would drive to the bank with two banking chores, take care of one, and completely forget to do the other one. She would run to the minimart for three items and then wouldn't remember what they were when she arrived there less than five minutes later. Was Elaine going to deteriorate just like her mom?

Her ten-year-old son Chad did very poorly in school. Already he had been held back a year, and it might happen again. In contrast, her daughter Stephanie shone scholastically—so much so, in fact, that she had skipped eighth grade and at age thirteen was already a high-school freshman. But the poor child suffered frequent headaches.

To top it off, Elaine had read recently that if large portions of a person's normal childhood memories are blocked out, intense abuse may have been present, abuse that adversely affects that person throughout life. Her husband Ron could not remember a thing about his growing-up years. He possessed an overactive libido and an underactive concern for tomorrow. What was going on here?

"You see?" Ron told her. "You read too much and so you worry too much. If you'd just relax, everything would work out fine. Why don't you kick off your shoes and hang out?"

"You sound like Dr. Gross," Elaine said. "Ron, I'm not worrying too much. I've learned to handle worry. If I'm starting to go the way Mom went, I want to prepare now. And I can't see how Stephanie's headaches or Chad's poor school performance would improve if I suddenly quit concerning myself with life and got a job weaving hammocks in some commune."

"Our problems aren't big ones," Ron said. "No one's dying of cancer or anything. Nobody in jail that I know of."

"Problems don't have to be big to be problems, Ron." Elaine stared out the window a few moments at their backyard. The leaves needed raking, and Chad's cockamamy building projects were strewed all over, as usual. "But they could become big problems. This sleeplessness . . . and forgetfulness . . . and the kids. Ron, I'm so scared."

The Importance of Memory

Elaine had every right to be frightened of the future. Ron could be headed for disaster if his memory blank really was a sign of something serious, and the prospect of Alzheimer's and obesity plagued Elaine's tomorrows.

She didn't know it at first, but by understanding how memory works, realizing what it will and will not do, and then acting on that understanding, Elaine Houser could reshape much of her and her family's future, and that includes many aspects of health. The techniques she would use can improve anyone's life, even the lives of those lucky souls for whom it seems nothing ever goes wrong and everything comes up roses.

Health problems often can be reduced without medication by examining memory. I'm not saying that every health problem is linked to memory. Of course, germs and disease and random physical damage strike us all. But an amazing number of health problems can be eased or eliminated by working with memory, problems that you would not at first associate with memory.

Terrible memories? You can do much to ease them.

Poor memory? You can do much to improve it.

No memory at all? We will explore several possible reasons. In my practice I frequently find people who are plagued by repeated self-destructive actions that all go back to memories that have never reached their conscious minds.

Does that sound frighteningly powerful? Memory is! Your brain is composed of about fourteen *billion* nerve cells. Each cell connects with all the others in from five hundred to five thousand different ways. Your brain has more possible connections than there are stars in our galaxy. My friend Dr. David Seamands pictures the brain as a network of telephone switchboards serving all the major cities. The switches instantly connect the thousands of calls that go through every moment—some local, some long distance.

Those interconnections are working in there all the time, building dreams (and nightmares!), making inferences, and collating information. They're directing actions and developing some skills while letting others slide. They are making associations both expected and unexpected. And they're storing, storing, storing everything your conscious mind picks up.

"Not my brain," you say. "I can't remember where I left my car keys an hour ago. I can remember the New Year's Eve party at my best friend's house in Cleveland back in '83, and the wonderful corned beef on the buffet, but I can't remember another soul of the twenty people who also attended."

Ron Houser's neighbor across the street, Gay Strom, had just the opposite problem. A widow of about sixty-five, Gay lived alone in a dim little duplex. She didn't much like her renters in the other half of the duplex, but they paid the rent on time. She suffered serious health problems, heart irregularity and colitis among them. She had few friends. Gay Strom carried grudges. She could remember wrongs done to her for years and years. Most people do to some extent, but she carried the memories in exquisite detail. She could recite chapter and verse of every slight ever done her, every overcharge and incident of price chiseling (however minor), every misquote by a careless neighbor.

Some of the wrongs were serious and worth remembering; others were absolutely nonsensical. On one occasion she returned home and walked in on burglars. She ran next door, met a locked door, and had to run across the street to the Housers'. The burglars escaped as she was seeking a phone. She never forgave the renter next door for not being home that day. If that person had been home, she reasoned, she would have reached a phone in time. In fact, the burglars might not have struck in the first place. You see? Nonsensical.

Gay didn't want to be like that. She wanted desperately to be able to put away some of her hurts. She couldn't. She would forgive, but she couldn't forget.

It's there. Everything's there, for better or worse.

As you explore some of the many ways that your memory shapes and directs you, you can begin to see what a powerful thing memory is. By the close of this book you will be able to better tap into that power.

Understand the Power of Memory

Elaine studied her ten-year-old son. *I read somewhere that we use only 1 percent of our mind's capacity. I think Chad turned part of that 1 percent in for a refund.*

Out in the backyard, Chad was ignoring the muggy afternoon heat to build the Housermobile. The Housermobile's chassis was a battered wooden wagon Chad bought for fifty cents at a garage sale. He formed a body with standard one-inch lumber scraps and fashioned a windshield with a carefully shaped coat hanger. He then created windshield wipers out of wire, even though there was no glass.

From inside the house Elaine could see the rivulets of sweat on her son's brow, pasting down his stray wisps of hair. *Why can't he devote a tiny bit of that energy to schoolwork?* she thought.

Actually, the estimate of 1 percent Elaine quoted is probably optimistic for everyone, not just Chad. It's likely less than 1 percent. This isn't just the capacity to remember details, facts, and events. It's also the ability to remember how to get to various places and how to do various things. Even more important, it's the record of our emotional lives and it rules how every person thinks and acts.

The initial step toward managing and using memory is to grasp how powerfully it works in your life. You have done that to some extent. Now I urge you to further explore the influences of memory on your life.

Grasping the Scope of Memories

"Ron's father is in a nursing home," Elaine said as we discussed her family. "He suffered a series of ministrokes that damaged scattered parts of his memory. You know what's weird? He lost his ability to walk because he didn't always remember to move his left leg. He'd take a step with his right leg and everything would stop until Mom reminded him to move his left." She wagged her head. "He's in failing health generally, but that one little thing always disturbed me the most."

One crucial bit of memory was erased with far-reaching consequences.

The effects of memory are so pervasive that you use memory even when you travel somewhere you've never been or do something you've never tried. Your memory still directs your efforts. When your mind encounters an unfamiliar situation, it instantly sorts through the memory files for a similar situation. It then uses the familiar to make sense of the unfamiliar.

For example, you have just rented a car in Ireland, but you have never driven on the left side of the road. For the duration of your stay in Ireland, all of your driving skills and reflexes must be mirror images of what is normal for you. Your very life depends on it. You check out the car and find all the controls. Frankly, you're stalling a little. You're not afraid exactly, but you sure are hesitant about plunging in.

Time to go. A right turn out of the lot will send you into Dublin. You turn left. You are not about to take the final test of city traffic before you have passed a few pop quizzes. So you head for a rural road to practice turns and parking in a safe situation.

Within a day or two your confidence allows you to tackle city driving comfortably. You can handle passing (*overtaking*, in Ireland), traffic circles—thousands of them—cryptic traffic signs, and parallel parking in the narrow streets. You're even doing well with Gaelic place names. When you see *Baile Atha Cliath*, you know that's Dublin, even though you can't pronounce it.

Everything is going great until an approaching cattle truck forces you off the road, and you automatically turn to the right, not to the left—the correct way in Ireland. You sit there praising God that an accident was averted, but you're puzzled and disappointed by your incorrect response. You were successfully reprogrammed to the new way. Why did your mind revert at the moment you needed it most?

At the close of your tour, as you turn the car in, you feel a certain smug and heady pride in your accomplishment. You pulled it off. You rose to the challenge. Along with pride you feel a host of other emotions associated with the trip. How you delighted in the rambles through Kerry! The magnificent National Museum, the coast of Donegal, the intriguing Giant's Causeway, and the wonderful castles all provide pleasant memories. You remember anger, too, generated by an isolated incident in Kilkenny. And will you ever forget the smell of freshly baked scones at that bed-and-breakfast near Drogheda?

From the beginning in that rental agency lot, those new situations were actually directed by your existing memory. You know what controls do in cars and where they are found on American vehicles. The steering wheels are on the left. Memory helped you locate them in their new orientation on the right. You already can read a map. Your memory used that existing knowledge to help you read Irish maps. Also, you have some dead-reckoning ability—*This way is south, so if I go in this direction, I'll eventually reach that east-west road*—and your mind was called upon from time to time to use it. Foreign country, strange surroundings, but north is still north.

To direct the new mirror-image skills required for driving, your mind called up its core knowledge, the things you have been doing for years, and adjusted it to fit the new circumstance. The more you reinforced those newly remembered skills through practice and repetition, the more firmly they were implanted. Thus, the skill became progressively easier and more natural feeling as you drove around the country.

However, that core knowledge was not altered; it was merely added to. Under stress, especially sudden stress, your mind does not take the time to sift through the recent changes. It goes right to the core memories that are embedded deepest by repeated reinforcement through time. Thus, you turned right, the ingrained response, to avoid that truck.

Moreover, the emotional memories and responses are tucked away in several other parts of your mind as well. The smell of scones may bring images of Drogheda back to you. But it may only bring back the emotional response, pleasure, as your conscious mind tries unsuccessfully to recall exactly where you smelled that aroma. An incident that superficially reminds you of what happened in Kilkenny makes you angry when anger is not an appropriate response at all. Myriad connections within your mind call up both the usual and the unusual, and we've scarcely begun to figure out what triggers those connections.

The more exotic a skill, the harder your memory has to work to fashion a new fit. What if you go to Australia (they drive on the left there also) and take an outback trip on camels? Even if your prior experience includes horses and ponies, your mind isn't going to find much of the familiar on which to base your newly required skill of camel handling. You will end up complaining, "The camel is smarter than I am," and that's not true. However, the camel does know everything there is to know about camels, and a little bit about other human beings with which it has dealt. That puts the camel way ahead of you.

Ah, but if you then go to Sri Lanka on an elephant trip, you have several bases of information to call up—horses, ponies, and camels. By the time you get to the water buffalo excursion in Bangkok, you won't have nearly as much trouble working with the new animal as you did with the camel. You have a broader base of varied memories from which to draw.

Your mind makes an endless variety of associations beyond verbal level, whether words are used or not. That is why you could handle those Irish place names even though you did not know the Gaelic language, could not pronounce the place names, and at times did not even know the names' English equivalents.

The example of driving in Ireland provides several clues about how your mind works and how memories are made. We will explore those clues in the chapters that follow and discover the many ways in which you can tap the wonderful power of your memory.

Everything you do or say is directed by your memory, as is everywhere you go. And this does not just apply to exotic experiences and places. Think about it. What guides you as you find your way to work or to the grocery store or to the dentist's office? Do you have to search diligently for your bathroom each time you get up in the morning, or do you remember where it is? Must you look through all the kitchen cabinets for the pan you want, or do you already have an idea where to find it? Why do you know to look in the kitchen for the cooking utensils? Why not the garage or the bedroom? Memory.

Getting Started

Elaine Houser had not arrived at a point of desperation, but she was concerned enough about her memory lapses, not to mention Ron's absence of recall, that she came to us for counsel. "Best to deal with this now," she said. "It's not going to get better."

"But you're not worried, right?"

"Right." She paused. "Wrong. I'm worried sick. I see my mom deteriorate and . . . and . . . and Ron! What if that's something terrible?"

"Then we'll get to the bottom of it," I said.

In the course of her visits we not only got to the bottom of her fears and worries, but we also achieved much more. We helped her children's lives run much more smoothly. That is one of the nicest things about working with memories—everything else gets better as well.

In this book we will explore how to make your personal

memories work better for you. We will also identify how memory may be working against you. If this is true for you—and just about all of us have some crippling memories—you will learn how to heal damaged and painful memories. You can actually turn bad memories into good ones or replace them with good ones. We will look at the reasons that some people cannot remember much from their childhoods. We will explore how you can tell that you are having a problem with painful memories, whether you are aware of them or not.

How can you learn to improve your memory? There is no one right way. "Different strokes for different folks," as they say, is extremely important in this area of learning.

Helping children remember well is as important to their well-being as providing good memories. We will discuss how to do both.

Why do you remember some details and not others? What determines what stays in mind and what gets buried? Can that be changed? What is the limit of what you can remember? How do dreams form? If you are interested in the fascinating data about memory and how to make it work, this book is for you.

To get started let's look at the brain, the relatively small organ that exerts such massive control on everything we do, and how it processes our experiences to form memories that never leave us.

2

Our Mind's Amazing Power to Remember

What word am I thinking of? Here are some clues:

- The corners of the mouth turn upward.
- "_____. You're on 'Candid Camera.' "
- "Let a _____ Be Your Umbrella."

I could just as easily have drawn a simple circle, put in it two dots for eyes, and drawn an upcurved line, and you would have caught on. In other words, a visual image would have been a good enough clue to bring the word *smile* to mind.

When we were doing the Minirth Meier New Life Clinic radio series on memories, Mike Frazier, the moderator, said, "I wish you could see the smile on Frank's face right now." I was smiling as I listened to a beautiful rendition of the classic gospel hymn "Precious Memories." That was an auditory image eliciting a fond memory along with its facial expression, a smile.

As that song played I was not thinking of any distinct incident or any particular person. I was not recalling any specific image at all. The extremely pleasant emotions accompanying that song were themselves the memory. With the appropriate trigger, you can recall emotions without the events or persons that first generated or accompanied them. In this case those pleasant memories were stored in my *long*-term memory banks. I heard that song frequently in my childhood.

The word *memory* takes in many different kinds of thought and concept storage. Understanding something about how this works will help you see how your own memories subtly manipulate you, and in turn how you can manipulate your memories. If you don't realize how memories are affecting you, you can't do much to control them.

There are three main types of memory: episodic memory, somatic data, and procedural memory.

Episodic Memory

"Did you ever go camping with a llama?" Elaine Houser's face twisted into a sort of I'm-sucking-in-vinegar-flavored-spaghetti pucker. You could sure read her mind without bifocals.

I could have truthfully told her, "I enjoy llamas; I own one." But I didn't. It was obvious she wouldn't have been impressed with my wisdom or intelligence.

She plunged ahead, eager to describe her torment and unburden herself. "What a horrible weekend! For one thing, it rained. That didn't seem to bother the llama, of course, but it was no fun for us. We were going to put all the camping gear on the llama, you see, and just enjoy hiking. Did you know llamas can only carry sixty pounds? We had to haul all this equipment."

"Tent and food, you mean."

"Right. And llama food, for crying out loud!" Elaine said. "Anyway, Ron thought handling a llama would be easy, sort of like a pony. It isn't. He got spit on twice, and he couldn't get it to go where he wanted, and it was terribly nervous all the time. The only person who really got along well with the llama was Chad. You know, now that I think about it, Chad and the llama shared a lot; they're both constantly active and hard to get along with, and so stubborn."

Obviously, Elaine's memory associations concerning llamas were vivid. My memories differ radically from hers. I think of our llama's wonderful, furry, soft, split lip, tickling as it nibbles grain off my open hand. I think of the huge brown eyes with long, rich black lashes. It nuzzles affectionately, follows me around the lot, and adores the kids.

Positive or negative, this sort of memory we call *episodic*. It's what you usually think of first when you think of "memory." You have a multitude of data stored in your own episodic memory. Pause for a moment and think of some event or incident that you experienced. It could be a party, a horseback ride, perhaps even a camping trip employing llamas, or the simple act of curling up in a soft chair with a good book.

What will first pop into Elaine's head the next time she sees a llama? In fact, those memories might surface if she sees a camel, because llamas and camels, being in the same family, share eye shape and other characteristics. They are similar enough to evoke the same memories. Are you beginning to see how every episodic memory shapes the perception of every future event?

Somatic Data

Now think for a moment about all the general knowledge you have accumulated. You don't think you've amassed very much? You have built a vast storehouse of tidbits over the years, not necessarily by any particular design.

Think of the score of things you know about wood. For example, it comes from trees, varies in hardness, can be burned, and its chips can be turned into particle board. That's the data you have already stored about wood. How do you know wood is a building material? You didn't set out to learn that. You know it is, more or less, because you know it is. We call that sort of thing *somatic generalized data*.

"That's my brother Glenn!" Elaine said, bobbing her head. "Unbeatable at Trivial Pursuit. He knows all these strange little facts no one else in the whole world gives a rip about."

"How about your immediate family?" I asked. "Ron and the kids?"

"Ron? He's so-so. The more recent the information, the better he retains it. Chad? Forget it. Chad refuses to learn stuff like that. I know he's only ten years old, but he doesn't begin to try. He can't tell you who won the Revolutionary War."

"And Stephanie is just the opposite?"

"If anyone has a chance to beat Glenn at Trivial Pursuit, it's Steph. He has the advantage of knowing more recent events because he lived it and she didn't. In a few years, though . . ." Elaine giggled. "Glenn will be history!"

The last type of memory is procedural memory.

Procedural Memory

"Elaine plays the piano beautifully," Ron said to me.

"What do you play?" I asked.

He looked slightly embarrassed. "Another keyboard instrument, actually," he said. "My parents sent me to accordion lessons when I was Chad's age. Want to hear 'Lady of Spain'?"

Ron and Elaine purchased for their children an elaborate electronic keyboard hoping to interest them in music. Chad played with it, but never to the point of learning to read music. Stephanie explored its possibilities, then drifted off to other interests.

"The keyboards she likes best are all attached to computers," Elaine said. "She loves computers."

Procedural memory is all the things you have learned how to do. Stephanie typed on a keyboard, and her parents played music on keyboards of a different sort because they had committed to memory the procedure for doing so.

Change a lightbulb. Milk a cow. Operate an automobile. Fire a gun. Bake a pie. Get from Irving, Texas, to Richardson without becoming stuck in rush-hour traffic. All these kinds of memory followed a similar path into your brain from the external world. They reposed temporarily in your short-term memory and then were distributed to other storage areas.

You have probably heard the terms long- and short-term memory many times. Yes, they do differ. In fact, there are three stages of memory. Sensory holding is the part of your brain that receives input from outside for processing. When the sense organs, such as eyes and ears, send information in, this is where they send it. The short-term memory, usually at work less than thirty seconds on any particular bit of information, processes the input from sensory holding in particular ways. Then the long-term memory takes over. But it does not end there. Once stashed, memories do not just sit. They are constantly being reworked below conscious level.

This reworking is a blessing, as you will see later. Because memories are not set in cement, memories can be improved and bad habits removed. Let's examine in detail how memories are processed through our short-term and long-term memories.

Short-Term Memory

Here's a random list of words: *yellow, basket, pencil, sit.* Without looking at the list again, can you repeat it? As another example consider these five numbers: 8, 3, 9, 6, 2. Without looking at them again, how many can you recite in the order they were given? Can you recite them backward?

I chose these words and numbers assuming that, taken together, they mean virtually nothing to you personally. However, let's say that you recently received as a gift a yellow basket designed to sit on your desk and hold pencils—which are usually yellow also. Suddenly, these four words bear intrinsic meaning for you personally. They instantly become extremely easy to remember. Random as they are to most people, they aren't random at all to you.

Similarly, if 83962 happens to be your zip code, it's not random and you have already memorized it. These nonrandom things skip past short-term memory because they are already in there somewhere, or relatively so.

Short-term memory is, specifically, the recall of unrelated items you received moments ago. Your short-term memory takes in many images, sounds, etc., every waking moment. Most of this input it disregards, particularly random information. It later chooses and shunts a few of those images off to long-term storage.

But that is a gross oversimplification, which does not tell the whole story. Think about the clues to the word *smile*, which began this chapter. One is a verbal description of a visual image. One is a commonly heard catch phrase from a popular television series. One is a song title as well as the song's first line. All of these are very different associations made from different, far-flung contexts. Had I drawn a simple smile face, that visual image is still another department, so to speak, of associations. And yet, they all instantly produce the desired word—*smile*. Are you beginning to see how intricately your memories are cross-referenced and cross-connected, and how well all those switchboardlike interconnections operate?

Three different processes engage in the making of your personal memories: *encoding, storage*, and *retrieval*. You can use each of the three processes in various ways to manipulate and manage memory. Encoding and storage, at least, begin well before birth, perhaps even before the third trimester of gestation. We do not know when a baby begins retrieving encoded and stored sensations, but we know it is very early. At birth a baby already knows its mother's voice.

The human mouth and voice are capable of about 150 different sounds. Some cannot even be reproduced with alphabet symbols. For example, certain African languages employ a clicking sound that we symbolize with an exclamation mark used like a letter. The English language is made up of perhaps half the possible range of sounds. By six months of age, a baby loses the skills for universal linguistics and disregards all except the sounds found in its native language. Babies born into one of the groups using these particular African languages can pronounce a word like *!kung* easily when they start talking. All other children cannot, at least not easily.

Babies a few months old can remember sequences and locations. They display an ability to remember quantities of objects and even to predict what should happen if you add one doll plus two dolls. In short, their short- and long-term memories are already working at full speed, right from the very beginning.

What, physically, makes a memory? How do sights, sounds, emotions, aromas, tactile sensations, tastes, thoughts, and impressions—in short, the totality of human experience—come to be recorded in a relatively small organ of flesh?

Encoding

Translating the memories from external sensation to internal record is the first step. This part is termed "encoding."

"No problem." Ron Houser was certain he had it all figured out. "It's like a video camera, except that it records tastes and touch and everything, as well as sights and sounds. You record the event, and if you have perfect memory, you can play it all back. Unfortunately, my video camera is on the fritz. It just dumps most of what it gets."

No, Ron. That's not quite the way it works.

What Goes On with Encoding

The connections between nerves are called *synapses*. A tiny impulse, partly electrical and mostly chemical, crosses the synapse to form a nerve linkage. Although each nerve cell in the brain has many synapses and the potential for many connections, few of these synapses actually fire. So, while the potential is great, the actual connections are much fewer.

Once an impulse crosses a synapse, the next impulse will cross much more readily. A path has been burned, so to speak, although the word *burned* is certainly inexact. The more these impulses cross a synapse, the easier such crossings become. This is what makes habits and thoughts ingrained. The memory has been replayed so many times, it's burned in deeply.

We have found that you can improve your memory significantly simply by using it. And, as both human beings and animals learn more things, the number of synapse connections actually increases.

My friend and colleague Paul Meier attests to that. "It used to take me forty-five minutes to memorize a Scripture verse," he said. "I kept at it. Eventually I got so I could memorize a whole chapter in forty-five minutes. It sounds illogical, because you think of the brain as a sort of bucket you fill up, and when it's full, it's full. But that's not how it is. The more you memorize, the easier it gets."

Diligent practice makes perfect.

Nothing illustrates this better than when Elaine plays the piano. She thought once of becoming a concert pianist, and she's good enough that she could probably do it. Think of the processes and connections her brain goes through. As she follows the printed score of a complex piece with her eyes, her hands are performing what her eyes see. Think how many cross-connections must occur almost simultaneously as eye and hand and printed music and piano are all brought together!

As a practiced pianist executes these fantastically swift runs of closely spaced thirty-second and sixty-fourth notes, the fingers may actually blur; they move too fast to clearly be seen. The more the pianist practices, the more quickly the synapses will transfer messages. The easier and more fluid—and faster—playing will become. Any concert pianist will tell you how extremely important are hours of *daily* practice.

"Wait," Elaine said. "You're not mentioning the biggest part of concert play, memorizing the music. A concert pianist has to memorize a large number of lengthy works."

Musicians agree that, in general, the more music they learn, the easier it is to commit additional music to memory. It's exactly the same process Paul Meier was talking about above, and it works not just for words or music, but for any endeavor.

Using Encoding to Advantage

What do you want to memorize? Work on it! Memorize more! Don't worry that you might fill up the barrel and have no more room for information. The more you try to fill the barrel, the bigger the barrel becomes.

Picture Elaine picking up a piece of unfamiliar music and playing it through for the first time. Eye and hand are well accustomed to working together, but still, they must coordinate in new ways. The music must be encoded from printed page to nerve synapses.

Sensory holding takes in the raw data. The eyes look at the notes and send the images to the brain. In a sense that is the first coding, as physical ink on physical paper is translated into nerve impulses. With time, through repetition and pattern recognition, Elaine first learns to play the music well and eventually memorizes the entire piece.

The Sifting Process

Memory encoding happens first in the short-term memory, and it is that aspect of memory which comes closest to Ron's comparison to the video camera. Still, the idea of a rote recorded image falls far short. This fact is important for several reasons. One is that, because your memory does not work like a video camera, there are blank spots in memories that you and others can fill in later. Can you alter actual memories? Yes. The second reason is that the things your memory filters in a given situation may not be what other persons filter. For better or worse, your perceptions are uniquely yours. As we will see, that can hinder you from seeing someone else's point of view. Here is how encoding sifts out information.

A series of stimuli picked up by ears, eyes, organs of touch, the tongue, and the olfactory organs (by which you smell odors) all register in the brain through their attendant nerves. Sensory holding shoots these impulses to the short-term memory. Immediately the brain sifts out anything unusual among the impulses and virtually disregards the rest.

For example, while you read the beginning of this chapter, what was going on around you? Were you sitting at home, on a bus, or in a library? Were the kids around? What was cooking on the stove? These things all stimulated the appropriate sensory organs, but the brain filtered them out as unnecessary details. It's doing so this minute. Are you breathing? Did you notice your breathing before I mentioned it?

Think about a rosebush. Specifically, a double tea rose, two-tone cream and magenta. What do you envision? Now think about what a photograph of the bush would record. The photo would show mostly green. When the size and volume of the flower is compared to the size of the bush with all the leaves, the flower is not a significant part. Even if it is blooming profusely, the bush is still mostly foliage. The flower would take up a very small part of the photograph. Yet it's the flower we remember, appearing bigger and more beautiful in memory than it actually is, not the whole photographic image. And of course, the photo cannot conjure up the heady aroma of a tea rose in full bloom. In other words, our brain sifts for the item of interest—the item of focus—and reduces the rest. Even if you were looking at the actual rosebush, you would not notice how many leaves it has or that some of them are infected with a fungus unless you are a horticulturist attuned to such things.

When Elaine would scold Chad (Stephanie too, for that matter) about an event in which he committed some infraction, he might not notice the error that angered her. This is why children often "see" and remember things from a trip or situation that the parents don't recall at all. And vice versa, of course. Their brains are focused on entirely different elements of the situation.

As the brain sifts selectively, it is also sorting. It places what it receives into patterns and categories and immediately relates them to other patterns and categories. How often have you said, "Oh, yes! That reminds me . . . ," about something seemingly altogether unrelated? Your brain made an arcane cross-reference, and the similarity, however unlikely, popped to conscious mind.

Incidentally, without looking, can you still remember the four unrelated words I placed at the front of the chapter? How about those five numbers? They were put in your short-term memory as you read. The short-term memory, moreover, is limited. Again we are oversimplifying the process, but in essence, as you stuff more into it at one end, it starts dumping things out the back end. That is why if you receive a long list of random items, you will be able to recall the final items of the list more easily than you can remember the first ones. We call the holding capacity of the short-term memory the *memory span*. We believe that most people's short-term memory span is about seven unrelated items. That's a telephone number. That is also why the zip-plus-four is hard to remember. A basic zip code of five digits most people can handle easily. Nine is typically over the limit.

"There! See?" Elaine said. "That's my problem right there.

My memory span is as short as a bug's toenails. In one end and out the other, boom boom, that quick."

Were the four items at the start of the chapter clearly related or the five numbers part of an arithmetic sequence, you could remember them without difficulty. They would form an easily grasped pattern. 2, 4, 6, 8, 10. You could recall that anytime. Your brain identifies it with an established pattern. After all, you were counting by twos and doing the times-two multiplication table back in third grade. If the pattern already exists, therefore, your memory immediately processes that fact.

To help make a random series stick in your short-term memory, rehearse it several times. Pianists play daily for hours, making the music stick. Likewise, as you repeat the series over and over, you are in essence reinserting it into your short-term memory. The more the short-term memory receives it, the more readily it sends it over into the long-term memory.

The long-term memory is what helps you ride a bicycle fifteen years after the last time you rode one. Ah, but do you remember the analytical geometry that you learned as a sophomore in college? Or the trig in high school? How does a sine relate to a tangent? Do you even remember what sines and tangents are?

Ron said, "Well, yeah. As a matter of fact I do. You see, I use trig a lot at work. It's handy for triangulating the heights of trees and buildings. It's good for a lot of things. Sure, you can measure more carefully, right to the millimeter, with fancy electronic gadgets, but a couple trig functions and a tape measure can give you a darned close estimate."

Ron took Spanish in high school and German in college. "I can't remember a word in German except *gesundheit*. Okay, I remember 'O Tannenbaum' too. But I can speak Spanish all right." Ron uses Spanish frequently because his company does business in Latin America. And he remembers the only two German words he's used since college, at Christmas and whenever someone sneezes. Practice and rehearsal play an important part in how well your long-term memory retains information in a place where you can retrieve it.

Storage and retrieval, the other two elements of memory, are so important I will discuss them at length in chapter 3. Encoding information is only a third of the memory process. You have to hang onto the stuff and be able to get it back. How you go about that can make the difference between the good use of memory and the poor and even physically damaging use of it.

Test the Power of Your Memory

Before we move on, however, you might like to assay what a wonderful thing your memory already is by building a list specific to you. No need to write it all down. It would take forever. Rather, just review in your mind the various items. Put your recall on fast forward when you can. The purpose is to remind yourself how much you already know and how memory permeates every moment of your day. Here are some suggestions to get you thinking:

Things you remember how to do:
- Everyday skills, from dressing to setting the table
- Skills you have amassed; sports, hobbies
- Skills you perform at work, whether rarely or routinely
- Other skills and processes

People you know whom you have not seen in over a year:
- Relatives
- Friends
- People with whom you associate poor memories; people you don't like

People you see and recognize every day:
- Family
- Friends
- Coworkers

Recalling past events

Dwell upon the details of three pleasant incidents that occurred at least five years ago. They needn't be of compelling importance, just happy little memories.

Now dwell upon three unpleasant moments or incidents (ever get a speeding ticket? Suffer loss in a storm? Argue?). Spend a few moments reflecting on how these isolated incidents are such a small part of your memory trove.

Orientation

Pick twenty locations at random and mentally rehearse how you would get there and back. They can be anywhere from the corner mailbox to a friend's house on the other side of the country, travel involving a few steps or several changes of airplanes.

Brief survey of facts

As indicative of the ocean of information you've stashed in your memory, scan how much you know about a few tiny little subjects, little embayments in the big sea.

Choose a foreign country you have never visited and come up with ten facts about the country and its people that you picked up in school or somewhere else.

Figures

Quote from memory at least one number that pertains to you, such as a social security number.

To yourself, recite five telephone numbers besides your own that you know by heart.

Write down five random numbers. Now see how fast, in separate arithmetic exercises, you can a) add all five, b) subtract the smallest from the largest, c) find the mean (that is, average the five), d) divide any one of them into any other one, and e) multiply any two of them.

Consider how many separate gyrations your memory had to go through and how much it had to call up to perform the above functions.

Now look at one more aspect of your memory. Quite probably you did not just randomly multiply any two and divide any two. Quite probably, some of your mental activity performing the above functions was devoted to choosing which of the five to multiply and which to divide to make the functions go as fast and as easily as possible. We do that kind of choosing and sorting all the time in real life.

The list is pretty impressive, isn't it? And you've not even scratched the surface. Every single function of memory we have surveyed above, and countless more besides, have shaped you, making you what you are right now.

3

The Changing World Inside Our Memories

Chad Houser, inventor of the Housermobile, sat in class while Mrs. Mason discussed nouns, wondering what color he ought to paint the trim on his Housermobile. Obviously the body color would be red, but what about the wheels and interior? Could they be red too?

"Chad! Can you answer the question?" Mrs. Mason asked.

"Red!" Chad shouted.

"Very good, Chad," Mrs. Mason said. "I'm surprised. I didn't think you were listening. Red is an excellent example of a word that can be either a noun or an adjective. Holly, can you use *red* as a noun?"

Chad sat kind of dumbfounded and muddled. He grinned. Hey, one way or another, he got it right. But his interests were not limited to creating wooden autos. He was into rain forests too. Social studies and geography were the part of the school day that he liked best because right now they were studying rain forests. He thought about little poison arrow frogs that are red and black. He could paint the Housermobile interior black. Park a frog on his car and it would blend right in. He giggled out loud at the thought.

Mrs. Mason was not amused.

Chad (and we'll get into this at length in chapter 12) had a storage and retrieval problem that was intrinsic within him. He did not deliberately daydream. His brain went that way without him wanting it to. It retrieved information in haphazard ways.

You may well know children and adults like Chad who cannot keep their minds focused on the subject at hand, who come up with ingenious answers to problems, who score the most outrageous puns and non sequiturs. You wonder to yourself, "How did he think of that?" or "Whatever put *that* into her head?"

An examination of the storage and retrieval system will help us to understand that person.

The Storage System

"Storage? Sure." Ron's memory lesson continued. "On the wrinkly surface of your brain are all these little pictures, like a computer disk only more extensive, waiting to be remembered. Some of them are in a place where you can recall them quickly, and others are more remote, you might say."

Nope. That's not quite it, Ron.

What Gets Stored

Memories are not recorded rote even from the very beginning. I mentioned how your short-term memory processes incoming information from the very beginning, sifting out routine elements of your surroundings. The information is processed again as it enters the long-term memory as well.

The short-term memory can be sidetracked so that it forgets the information it just received. Time might erase the memory before it reaches long-term storage. We call that *decay*. One of Elaine's fears was that her brain was deteriorating because decay occurred too often and too quickly. For example, she sometimes forgot a list of a very few items within five minutes.

Something can override the short-term memory and replace it. Let's say you are going to send a letter and just looked up a familiar address. Before you can write it down, someone comes in and speaks to you. Now you have to look up the address again, because—zip!—the zip code has vanished. We say the conversation *interfered*. Decay and interference remove a lot of short-term memory before it ever reaches long-term storage.

However, Ron's concept of little pictures all over the brain surface is right in one regard. When certain areas of the brain are artificially stimulated, for instance with a probe by a surgeon, a person can remember whole scenes and events as if they were happening at that very moment. The memory is intact and complete.

This suggests that every detail of every experience ends up somewhere in the long-term memory, though the detail—and often the experience itself—is not accessible to recall.

"I remember a birthday party when I was twelve," Elaine recalled. "My father was what they called a home handyman. I remember he really hurried to finish a brick barbecue grill so it would be ready for the party. It was real smokey because the chimney didn't draw quite right, but it worked well enough. Neat party, good weather. But, you know, I cannot for the life of me remember who attended. Not a soul. I remember that barbecue grill, and even the cake, but not the guests."

Her situation is typical. You remember in vivid detail certain aspects of an experience and lose others. Moreover, you might even think that the part you lost is more important than the parts you remember. Today she had no interest in the barbecue grill as such. She wanted to recall her playmates.

Our brain, then, filters memories, sometimes causing them to be inaccurate. This happens because of *interest and emotion, distortion*, and *denial*.

Interest and Emotion

A lot of work has been done on how the brain sorts and categorizes information so it accesses it quickly and easily. To summarize our findings, we believe the brain stores processed information not in just one way, but in a variety of ways. To understand what is going on, let's invent a false memory.

Let's pretend that at the age of ten you and your family visited the annual Date Festival in Fresno, California. You had your first (and last) taste of goat cheese in a restaurant called the Caravansary. You and your brothers rode a carousel, the Octopus, and a real live camel. Now, thirty years later, what do you remember?

Your sharpest memories are of some of the things that attracted your eye and interest as a ten-year-old. The camel ride. The Octopus. The carousel and ferris wheel were fun but tame. You remember vaguely that there were displays in big buildings, maybe, but you can't recall what. Your parents, however, recall the displays vividly because they are both country people who grew up loving the county fairs. The Date Festival is a big, glorified regional version of the county fair, so your parents could tell you many details of the huge displays presented in the agricultural hall by major date and citrus growers.

As they described them, a vague recollection would emerge from your own memory, but it would be strongly colored—in fact, in important ways *created*—by your parents' verbal descriptions. The line between your own memory and your parents' description would blur, and your "original" memory of the event would contain elements placed in it at the actual time by you and also in the present time by your parents. If your parents' description was false or faulty, you would see and remember those citrus displays very clearly, *according to the false information*. In effect, your parents would have built an untrue recollection into your memory.

You remember the camel ride vividly and recall quite well the way you halfway developed motion sickness by the time the ride ended. Camels sway a great deal as they walk, like a rocking boat. And they smell. So did the goat cheese. That's why you've never had it again.

You remember the pleasure of the day and the positive emotions as you shared the occasion with your parents. You also remember seeing a five-year-old child standing by a trash barrel crying. The child had been separated from his parents, so your own folks took him to Lost and Found. You remember the child's reunion with his parents, and the sympathetic emotional impact of that event within an event has stayed with you. To this day, lost children tug especially hard at your heartstrings.

Your brain, then, recorded the event, or at least major elements of it, and stashed that memory somewhere you cannot tap into clearly. The sensations of the camel ride are easily accessed, and you can hardly see a camel without thinking of it. You certainly cannot smell a camel, as at the zoo, without remembering it. The brain stored the camel ride as a unit in places where sights, smells, and sometimes nothing at all can call it up. Your emotional responses of that day were stored in places where they can be accessed independently of the rest of the event. In short, as that event entered your long-term memory, some parts remain easily accessible three decades later. Some parts have slipped away. Some can be rejuvenated, changed, improved, and even created by recent input (your parents). And some, such as the lost child, are called up by stimuli at times you don't expect.

Now perhaps you can see why Elaine's memories of that party are so selective. When she actually experienced the event, the guests were all good friends and schoolmates. They were already familiar; there was no need to give them special memory emphasis at the time. That barbecue grill, however, was a whole different matter. She watched her father and mother invest a lot of hours, interest, and effort in it. She helped them. Everyone worked to have it ready in time. It stood in a place by the grape arbor that had been empty until then. In several different ways, therefore, it stood out. Her short-term memory sifted out the event's unique features and sent it on, just the way your mind is probably filtering out most of your surroundings right now. Her long-term memory sorted its elements and stored it in several different contexts.

Today, she still finds the smell of smoke pleasant. Although the smell usually doesn't evoke the memory of the birthday party itself, the emotional context is brought to mind. A brickwork barbecue grill or any brickwork piece that looks superficially like it (including a brick oven in a pretzel bakery, which she saw during a tour in Pennsylvania) might bring the grill and/or the party to mind. Were her brain to be probed and the exact spot stimulated, quite possibly the whole scene would return to mind in complete detail. It's in there someplace. But she can access only bits and pieces.

Interest, then, is a major factor in how the brain will treat information, dismissing some elements and retaining others. Emotion is another. Memories and mood feed on each other. A positive mood creates positive memories, and a negative mood creates negative memories. Intense emotional experiences will produce intense memories that are vivid, detailed, and long lasting. Moreover, positive emotions do more than negative emotions to facilitate the memorizing process itself. Interest and emotions influence what the brain sifts out to save and how it will save it.

Distortion

Another way in which your brain filters the long-term memories it stores is what we call *distortion*. The brain distorts a memory by changing its shape, in a sense, to fit a shape already implanted in the brain by experience or surroundings—the culture and subculture you grow up in.

You recall that a baby is born being able to master any of the 150 possible speech sounds of human beings. By the age of six months the baby becomes attuned only to those nuances of the native language, the language the baby hears. Similarly, adults alter memories to fit certain cultural expectations. This is why status and saving face are so important to persons raised in some cultures and mean very little in other cultures. One culture takes care of murderers by executing them. Another simply ostracizes the murderer. In that culture the exclusion from society is sufficient punishment akin to death. Neither culture can appreciate fully the feelings of the other. This deeply ingrained cultural attitude is what shapes every memory.

Researchers explored the brain's unconscious cultural filter by reciting a particular story from a Northwest Indian culture to a non-Indian. They then asked the non-Indian to repeat it three days later. The non-Indian omitted certain details that did not ring true, so to speak, in her own culture, and added details that were culturally relevant to her but did not fit the culture from which the story arose. Those details were not in the story she heard. She had no idea she was adding anything. She was relating the story as faithfully as she could.

You are aware that you cannot translate a story directly from one language to another and get all the little nuances. But it goes far deeper than that. The differences the non-Indian inserted without realizing it were not differences of translation. The story was conveyed only in English. Rather her mind filtered the memory so that it would fit the cultural expectations she didn't even know she had.

We all filter every memory through a cultural sieve.

"Are you sure?" Elaine asked. "I don't belong to a culture as such. I'm just plain old suburban American, you might say. I mean, not a minority or anything."

The predominant culture in an area, the attitudes and perceptions of the people who surrounded you as you grew up, is certainly still a culture. Just so that you are aware of how your memories are culturally filtered, I suggest that you sharpen your awareness of your own cultural biases. Remember that *every* person has them; no one is free of cultural bias. Think about your own ancestral bias.

- My parents' race
- My parents' religions (be as specific as possible)
- My parents' economic strata (Lower class? Middle class? Upper class?)
- My parents' professions
- Their geographic home area
- Their immediate neighborhood (Affluent? Average? Squalid? Rural?)
- Any serious problems or dysfunctions (alcoholism, etc.)

Lastly, for each parent individually (and stepparents in addition, if appropriate), rehearse in your mind what you perceive that person's attitude is toward other races; other socioeconomic groups; religion; education; the earning and use of money; crime and punishment; dress and behavior; music and entertainment; the arts; sports; and hobbies.

Now repeat the exercise top to bottom for yourself. When you get to the last item, address each of the topics given. Be honest. You can destroy your paper after the exercise is completed if you wish, but examine your real cultural biases.

There is one more step. Finally, look again at what you believe your cultural biases to be. Examine how your memories affect the bias. Yes, the bias shapes your memories, but your memories shape the bias as well; it's an interactive situation. The strongest memory influence will be the bias you picked up from your parents. It infiltrates in a million ways below conscious level: observations, feelings, unspoken thoughts, the spoken word, attitudes revealed nonverbally through facial expressions and gestures. The youngest child picks these up. The next strongest influences will be your specific memories.

"Interesting," Elaine said. "I was about six, and my cousin Annie was nine or ten. I hung on every word she said. We were sitting on a fire escape behind her townhouse, I remember, and she told me the most terrible stories. They were about blacks; she called them [a racial slur]. I was shocked and fascinated. For years I wondered if her stories were true."

Elaine went through the above exercise examining her aunt, uncle, and cousin, and she found where those stories came from. And when she studied her own deepest cultural attitudes, she saw an influence by these people that was stronger than she realized.

Can Elaine—for that matter, can *you*—alter the filter? Absolutely. Being aware of it is the first and best way to prevent it from shaping your memories in ways you don't want.

The Wall of Denial

Another filtration the mind makes automatically is denial. Bad, painful memories are not stored in the same way as happy, pleasant memories. The painful memories are stored behind a protective wall which prevents easy access so that they don't continue to hurt constantly. I didn't say bad memories don't exert major influence. They certainly do. But they don't easily emerge into the conscious level.

These filters erode our memories. Yet we can combat some of that erosion.

How to Combat Erosion

Rehearsal and repetition aid long-term memory recall immensely. For example, how many presidents are depicted on Mount Rushmore? Who are they? In what order are they portrayed? Nearly everyone has a general idea based on pictures in schoolbooks. You will remember these details much better, though, if you have been there. They will be imprinted more clearly on your long-term memory because the sculpture was impressed upon you in more than one form of experience. An encyclopedia picture of it is one form, viewing it "live" out in the open air is another, hearing a taped presentation about it is still another, and the take-home literature from the park is yet another.

Simply rehearsing information over and over or periodically reviewing it helps to cement it in mind. This is why Ron can remember trigonometry and Spanish when most people who took those courses in school cannot. He uses them.

"Ah," said Ron. "That must be why my CPR card is only good for a year and the first-aid card is good for three. I'm supposed to take the refresher courses periodically so that I remember better."

Exactly. Repetition. Rehearsal. Just like the concert pianist.

Repetition reverses erosion. Memories erode (and are distorted) for several reasons, and we will explore those reasons in detail in chapter 5. Experts argue about whether the memory itself erodes or only the triggers which bring a memory to conscious mind are lost. Memory and its triggers can be erased by physical damage to the brain. Elaine's father's ministrokes are a case in point. Something like that cannot be averted or reversed. An accident, a misstep, a disease—they happen.

Erosion also occurs with age as brain cells die from various causes. When information is not brought to the fore frequently, it tends to fade. This is why you cannot remember certain school courses well if you never use the material you learned from them. One important factor reduces erosion of this sort: if you learn something that really interests you, it tends to stay with you better, probably because it is stored in more areas. A person with a major interest in history will remember dates and data that persons without a strong interest in history soon forget.

Medical doctors can retain large quantities of information couched in long words because we have an intense interest in the material. In many regards, this is our life. If we are to help people, we have to know these things. "How do you remember all that?" then, is a relative question, and people will sometimes ask me that very thing. Actually, a lot of things in which I have little or no interest come my way, and I don't remember them. But I remember medical information because it's important to what I do every day.

Some people, like Elaine's brother Glenn, simply enjoy trivia for trivia's sake. They take delight in it and therefore have no trouble accumulating all kinds of tidbits of information. Their interest in facts helps them retain large quantities of what many people would call "useless information."

"I'd love to have a memory like Glenn's," Elaine said. She paused, then added, "I don't know what I'd do with it, but I'd love to have it."

A woman I know just delights in greeting people with some esoteric question. "Hi, Frank," she'll say. "Who was Isambard Kingdom Brunel?" And if you don't happen to know that he was a famous engineer of the last century who built railways, bridges, and steamships (notably the *Great Eastern*, for years the largest vessel afloat), she'll tell you. Extensively. She thinks she's advancing knowledge. Most of her friends say she's driving them nuts.

These methods of combatting erosion help us to retrieve our memories.

Retrieval

"I can't remember names and faces to save me," Ron said. "My father has to wear a carnation in his lapel when he meets me at the airport."

The brain employs two kinds of information retrieval, and Ron has trouble with the kind called *recognition*.

Recognition

Recognition is picking out familiar items from among a body of items that includes some unfamiliar ones. His example of finding a person at the airport is good. Here are hundreds of people, almost all of them strangers. From that group Ron must pick out a familiar face—his father's. (And no, his father doesn't really have to make himself conspicuous by wearing a carnation. However, Ron is notoriously bad at recognizing casual acquaintances.)

In classic recognition experiments, researchers give the subject a list of items. Later, the researcher gives the subject a longer list containing some of the items on the first list plus a lot of items the subject didn't see before. The subject is supposed to pick out the familiar items from the longer list.

Retrieval of this sort tends to last long and well. You may not be able, for example, to recall certain names and faces out of thin air, but you can recognize them years later in a photo or in person, assuming they have not changed too much with time. You don't have to remember them in sequence or in patterns. You don't have to correlate them with much other information. You need only store the images, and you don't have to remember the images until one comes up.

Try to estimate how many people you have met in your lifetime. Of these people, how many do you actually think about? A very small proportion, I'll bet.

Recall

The other form of retrieval is *recall*, in which the brain retrieves information stored in it when asked to do so. For instance:

In which hand does the Statue of Liberty carry her torch?

Whose faces are chiseled into Mount Rushmore and in what order?

Describe the color we call *chartreuse*.

Recall is illustrated by the questions above. You are asked a question. You respond with the appropriate answer, assuming that you learned it in the first place and that you can recall what you learned.

I love asking about the Statue of Liberty. Almost everyone has seen a picture of it, and many have visited it. Probably everyone knows she carries the torch in her right hand. But when I ask the question, the responder suddenly loses confidence in the correctness of his or her reply.

"Well! I knew until you asked."

What is chartreuse? Answering that one depends not only on your knowledge of the correct response, but also upon your ability to express in words something that is essentially visual, a unique shade of green.

"Chartreuse? Uh, well, I know, but I can't explain."

How about the presidents on Mount Rushmore? Your mind immediately calls up images, either picture images or images from actually being there. The order of the presidents' appearance will pose a problem because that is something you must memorize. However, your brain can do a lot of good guessing to fill in missing information.

Let's assume you can't picture the scene clearly in your mind. To recall the identities of the four presidents, your brain sifts quickly through various cross-references concerning presidents that it knows and are readily at hand.

"Well," muses the brain's recollections, "surely Lincoln and Washington are there. Wouldn't be complete without them. And, uh . . . Jefferson? He was impressive, a true renaissance man. And, uh . . ." The brain is trying to reason out an answer not immediately in mind. It does that a great deal in obvious and not-so-obvious ways, all the time. You will probably miss Teddy Roosevelt if you miss anyone. The other three can be arrived at by guess, but their positions across the cliffside cannot be. That is something you just plain have to remember.

We call any stimulus that brings forth a memory a "trigger." In the cases above the questions are the triggers to call up information. They in turn pull other triggers, particularly when the brain is groping for an answer. Questions are not the most common triggers. Sight, sounds, smells (especially smells!), or other sensations can bring stored information to the conscious mind.

Consider the case of a man we will call Kevin. He watched his six-year-old daughter climb aboard the bus for her first day in first grade. A proud moment. Suddenly, inexplicably, he was flooded with hideous memories of cruelties perpetrated upon him in childhood by a trusted adult. He had not known such memories existed, and he doubted his sanity.

Where did those horrible memories of abuse and misery come from? What was the trigger that unleashed the flood? In Kevin's case, it was watching his child go off to school.

Kevin's family lived in a huge, three-story farmhouse ten miles outside of town. His father's brother, Uncle Homer, lived on the third floor and shared household costs and duties. One of the duties was minding preschooler Kevin while Mommy and Daddy went to work. Uncle Homer smiled and patted Kevin on the head while Mommy and Daddy were around. When they were gone, Homer teased Kevin sadistically and tickled or pinched him in ways that wouldn't show. He convinced Kevin that not only was it all Kevin's fault, but terrible things would happen if he ever breathed a word to anyone. A five- or six-year-old takes that kind of threat to heart instantly.

Kevin's escape was school. At school he was loved, appreciated, and treated kindly. At school, Uncle Homer could not reach him. Every morning Kevin looked forward eagerly to the bus that took him away for seven hours from that house of torture. The teasing and pinching ended only when Kevin, then a third grader, came home from school one day to learn that Uncle Homer had suffered a stroke. Uncle Homer spent the rest of his days in a nursing home, and Kevin got on with his own life, free at last of the pain and misery.

Kevin's brain sealed all those memories away where they could not hurt him. The denial was so complete that his brain had blocked off nearly all the triggers. Not even the name or image of Uncle Homer could evoke remembrance. You would expect memories of Uncle Homer to be obvious triggers. But Kevin's brain carefully suppressed those expected triggers. When Kevin recalled his uncle he pretty much came up with a blank. He thought nothing of it. A lot of people in our lives make little impression.

Parents possess a special bond with their children. To a certain extent, parents relive their own lives through their children. When the children do certain things or go through certain stages or rites of passage, the parents in a sense partake, not just as observers, but also as participants. When Kevin's little girl climbed aboard the bus, Kevin was not merely watching her depart. In his mind's eye, the six-year-old Kevin was also boarding the bus. That was the trigger, a stimulus Kevin's brain had not anticipated and, therefore, did not guard against.

Why then did Kevin have no such recollections for over twenty years? His own brain blocked out the record to save him from the pain. The memory was not erased. Such things never are. You will recall I mentioned that powerful emotions produce powerful memories. There is always a trigger for those memories somewhere, however carefully buried by our protective, survival-oriented unconscious.

Triggers can bring up not only a particular memory but a whole class of memories. Triggers may lump together a variety of different situations and treat them like one. We may not know that's happening. As the brain sorts and categorizes its memories, it uses the past as a guide to storing the present. When a new event occurs, the brain sifts through existing memories for an identical or similar experience as a guide to handling it. You do this all the time. However, when it hits a partial match, it may fail to distinguish between similar though different bits of programming. One trigger, then, retrieves more than one memory or response, and those other memories and responses might be totally inappropriate.

To illustrate, I remember a man who called in to our radio show when the series on memory first aired. The man's girlfriend had become pregnant and aborted the child against his wishes. He could not stop the death of his baby. Now he found himself unable to get close to any woman. His memories were preventing him from forming a close attachment. His brain was protecting itself against further pain.

At the time he called, getting close emotionally to a woman triggered the protective response: "Get back! Don't you remember? You were hurt once. It could happen again!" The events were not really similar at all, any more than the girlfriend in his past was similar to the women he subsequently met. In his case he needed to train his mind to distinguish between what appeared in his memory to be similar events. He needed to extinguish the association.

His bad memories, supposedly a lesson in how not to get hurt again, were preventing him from living a full life. In ways his conscious mind did not grasp, his memories shaped the way he behaved and even how well he got along in life.

Memories shape and delineate our very personalities. Kevin's personality was forever changed by his sadistic Uncle Homer. Elaine's life and Ron's—everybody's—would be different from what they are, were their memories different. Let's look at that next.

4

Memories—A Mirror of Who We Are

Sean Murphy is a leprechaun. By that I mean he is a professional leprechaun. He's a bit large as leprechauns go, standing about five feet five inches, but he's as Irish as shamrocks. He performs at wakes and parties doing a repertoire of magic tricks and singing. His big time of the year is St. Patrick's Day, of course, when he might work three parties a night for a week.

"Frankly, Frank," he confided one day, "I'm not satisfied being one of the wee folk. Sure, it's a living, but it's not lucrative. And my personal life is all gang topsal teery. I'd rather have someone who loves me than all the acclaim in Erin."

All gang topsal teery indeed. He was in his third marriage, with three children and eleven stepkids scattered across two states. Now this present marriage was about to break up, and Sean was desperate to save and stabilize it. His wife, Lilly, also was reluctant to end the marriage. But she was supplementing their income with her own job and claimed she didn't have time to attend "touchy feely sessions," as she called counseling. Her claim had much basis in fact; with four kids and a job, she didn't have any spare time. Still, she agreed to counseling as a last resort.

The fruitful use of memories came to the rescue. Both Sean and Lilly found the whole exercise fun as well as enlightening. You may wish to try it also for insight into your own personality.

The fundamental idea is simple. We call it the law of relative consistency. Out of our complete suite of memories, we pick those recollections of the past that are most consistent with our present attitudes and circumstances.

Our memories are a wonderful treasure chest, packed with good things. Good memories change our lives. I remember sitting on my mother's lap. Roaming in the woods with my dog. Riding horseback with my father. I remember hearing the grand old Bible stories when I was too young to grasp their immediate theological meanings—I just loved the stories as stories. Still do. And the hymns! The fine old hymns of the faith that I grew up with have literally shaped my life. They bring a new dimension to my faith in Jesus Christ. They give voice to "dry" theology. Those songs are among the deepest and most beautiful of my happy memories.

By reaching in to repack our memory now and then, we maximize the good. And by sorting around at the bottom, we can find out much about who we are now. So reach back as far as you possibly can into your memory trove and analyze what you see.

Early Memories

Most researchers agree that our personalities are pretty well shaped by the time we reach the age of four or five. Until and unless we deliberately step in and change things, this is the way we will respond to the world. This is the way we will forever view life. Memories shape our attitudes and our self-image.

Memories Shape Our Attitudes

Dr. Brian Newman, a psychotherapist at the Minirth Meier New Life Clinic, smiled as he related the differences between himself and his wife, Debi. "I see details," he said. "If any little thing gets out of its normal place, it stands out. I not only spot it immediately, it irritates me. Now Debi, she's the opposite. As long as it's there, she's happy; she doesn't care where 'there' is. The kids have toys strewn from one room to the other, and it doesn't bother her a bit. But it really irks me."

How do they compensate?

"We each have our space, somewhere, that's ours alone, and the other person doesn't comment about it," Brian said. "And we compromise about the common areas of the house. Toys picked up after a certain time, the place in order if company comes, that sort of thing. We've worked it out."

Almost never does a neatnik marry a neatnik. Herein lies the charm of the perennially popular concept of *The Odd Couple*.

"But neatness has nothing to do with memory," you may insist.

But does it?

What makes a neatnik a neatnik? There are two factors that influence people in these ways, and they both depend upon memory. Either the neatnik remembers an extremely neat childhood home and emulates it, or he remembers an extremely cluttered and chaotic childhood home and seeks to avoid it.

If you are married to a person of the opposite neatness persuasion or if you are the roommate of such a person, explore each other's backgrounds. What are the childhood memories pertaining to neatness and orderliness?

Childhood memories are so powerful and pervasive that they shape our personality from the very beginning. And neatness is only one aspect of that shaping. Childhood memories shape the way you think. It is not just left-brain/right-brain; it's also what is in the brain and has been there from the very beginning.

There is an important benefit to be gained from grasping how your childhood shaped the way you think. You then have the knowledge to reshape patterns, at least to an extent. Let's take neatness as the example, although the principle extends far beyond the simple matter of being neat verses being slovenly.

Look first at your mother's side of the family

- What sort of home did she grow up in?
- Did she enjoy a happy childhood? In other words did either the neatness or the chaos or the "averageness" she grew up in generate pleasant memories that she would wish to recreate?
- Did she have an easy time leaving home or a hard time? If her separation from her family of origin was fairly smooth (such separations are never totally smooth), she would not likely rebel against the kind of home she was raised in.

Do the same now with your father's side

- What sort of home did he grow up in?
- Did he enjoy a happy childhood?
- Did he have an easy time leaving home or a hard time?

And now, you

- What sort of home did you grow up in?
- Did you enjoy a happy childhood?
- Did you have an easy time leaving home or a hard time?

Keep in mind that most people eventually recreate the same kind of home life they knew in their childhood. They ultimately seek the comfort of the familiar, even if the familiar is most unpleasant. Do you see how memories can influence the kind of life you now need?

Another profound shaping element are the messages you received from early on. Messages in the memories of your past become prophetic unless you recognize them and deliberately alter them.

Memories Shape Our Self-Image

To explore the hidden messages buried in your memories, answer the following questions. Then ask yourself additional questions, for only you know your unique circumstances. But these will get you started:

- My mother [never] [sometimes] [often] expressed pride in my accomplishments.
- She [did] [did not] seem pleased with me.
- My father [never] [sometimes] [often] expressed pride in my accomplishments.
- He [did] [did not] seem pleased with me.

The following words describe what other people thought of you. For each word that applies, remember a specific situation or comment to illustrate it.

- Bright, intelligent
- Dull, stupid
- Average, middle of the IQ scale
- Creative, always building things
- Curious, always taking things apart
- Shy, withdrawn, hard to know
- Irritating, pesky, underfoot, in the way
- Cute, physically attractive
- Homely looking
- Either overweight or too skinny, abnormal build
- Other descriptions

Ponder your answers awhile. Think about how your memories of people's attitudes in the past may be affecting the way you think now, as well as your self-concept.

Now reverse it. Go through the questions above all over again. This time, deliberately answer the questions the opposite way. Try to come up with memories from your past to support this opposite viewpoint.

"No way!" you say.

You may be greatly surprised. For example, let's say you remember that your parents considered you a pest, always underfoot, and said so more than once. You wrote that down the first time through. This time, seek evidence that you were *not* a pest. Perhaps upon reflection you remember that your Aunt Sarah loved having you around and sometimes called your mother and asked her to send you to her house. Or perhaps you recall a teacher in your past who believed in you.

You cannot turn negative programming into positive programming. However, very frequently the negative messages in a person's memory overpower the positive ones. Strike a match and hold it near a 300 watt electric light. From three or four feet away the light of the match flame will be lost in the lightbulb's brilliance. The match is there doing its thing. You just don't notice it. It's that way with positive and negative messages as well.

Dig out the positive messages that run counter to the negative ones. Bringing them to light will do much toward helping you balance negative effects. And that is a key factor in altering bad memories.

Now let's look at your childhood memories. They reveal whether there is something in your life you don't like, and if so, exactly what about yourself you might want to change.

When Sean Murphy, the professional leprechaun, and I began to look at his memories, I asked him, "What was your earliest memory?"

"Which one?" he asked.

Good question.

Choosing the Memories

When choosing memories to analyze, pick the earliest ones you can dredge up. They are the most telling because they reveal the real you without any complications presented by later experiences. Also, try to bring up more than just one of these early memories.

"Ah. Me earliest. That would be when I was barely starting to walk. Me father's an archaeologist. Irish antiquities. He had his family along as he was excavating—a working holiday—and meself fell into Loch Gur. Near to drowned."

That one wouldn't count. That memory was hearsay; Sean's family described it so often that he knew all about the incident, but he himself could not recall it. The memories you choose to analyze must be yours alone.

"Mm. How about the time the whole family visited my dying grandfather. He spoke Gaelic, and that fascinated me. I was four, I'd guess. Every time he said something, I'd hide my head and repeat it. Didn't the family get a laugh out of that!"

Good. That was Sean's own recollection. The memories must involve specific events, not just blanket generalities, such as "We used to go for a walk in the park on Sundays." In that case you would want to analyze a memory of a specific incident that occurred during one or more of those walks, not just the vague concept that the family went out walking. For example, you might remember that one time a mean chow dog on the corner bit you.

Lilly, Sean's wife, recalled, "I used to wander in the woodland behind our home. We lived in Kerry, very near a forest preserve. I remember one day—and this was well before I started school— that I was on the path approaching the woods, and I stopped. For some reason I decided there was terrible danger in there. That was exceedingly strange because I spent a lot of time on that path. The woods were familiar to me. I loved them. But on that one occasion I turned around and ran home. And to this day I can't say why."

Later Lilly recalled another interesting memory. "I read all the A. A. Milne *Winnie the Pooh* books. I devoured them. Practically memorized them. Then I spent hours trying to get my stuffed bear to talk. I was really hoping he'd say, 'Oh, bother!' I was certain he could, absolutely certain, and he was just being obstinate. I remember that."

I asked how old she was then.

"Six, I'd say. I learned to read at four and a half and was easily reading that level of prose by the age of six."

How about you? Now is a good time to do a little self-analysis. What sorts of early recollections can you dig up? Don't worry about what they might reveal or fail to reveal. Just find the memories themselves, memories all your own.

Retrieving Your Memories to Identify Who You Are

When I help patients retrieve memories that show their personality, I walk them through a ten-step process.

1. Focus on the Incident

Sean bobbed his head. "Ye want a recollection that's clear? Our neighbor's potato soup. This delightful old lady in the street behind us made amazing potato soup. Potatoes, leeks, raw milk, garlic, a bit of ham. Meself would rap on her door and request some. Brazen I was as a lad! She'd scowl like an old witch, but a couple minutes later she'd hand a little bowlful out the door to me. And piping hot it was. I've no idea if she kept it on the back of her stove constantly or if she saw me coming. Ahh. Never have ye tasted the like of that soup!"

Although you might say that was not a specific incident, it was. Repeated, but specific. Sean's eyes lit up as he talked about that lady's soup. The recollection was vivid in his mind.

Both Sean and Lilly focused on the clearest part of their memories, which, not surprisingly, involved feelings.

What are the most vivid parts of the early memories you chose? Rehearse the memory a few times in your mind to bring it fully to the surface. Attach a feeling to the clearest part of your memory. Sean remembered utter delight, Lilly remembered fear. Regarding the incident at his dying grandfather's bedside, Sean recalled most clearly the curious mix of pleasure and embarrassment he felt when the other family members laughed at his actions.

What are your strongest recollections associated with that memory?

2. Analyze Your Memory

Lilly shrugged. "Either I was making up the danger altogether, or I sensed something that didn't reach conscious level, or my guardian angel was really on the ball that day. I'm not normally a scaredy-cat. I often walked in those woods alone. What's to analyze?"

Just that. *She often walked in the woods alone.* Note that in Lilly's memory she was alone. In her other memory, that of trying to make her bear talk, she was also alone. With both memories Lilly described the fruits of a vivid imagination. No, more than that. Vivid thought processes. In her earliest memories she already possessed a vibrant way of processing both fantasy and reality. She was a thinker.

Lilly shook her head. "There were many times I was not alone. Most times, in fact."

True! But those were not the earliest memories that came immediately to her surface recollection.

Most children possess remarkably similar memories of being

baby-sat, being at home or school, being alone, and being with others. Most people can remember frightening situations and warm, comforting situations. Each person has a broad gamut of memories hidden somewhere within from which to draw. But which ones were drawn? We are not looking for memories as clues to what happened in childhood but rather for what stuck best in easily-retrieved memory. Those memories that stuck, the memories on top as it were, are the keys to personality. They reveal the child's earliest attitudes.

Lilly could have remembered family parties or going to the shore or taking the train to Dublin with her cousins. Those things happened in her early years. However, if her sister had not reminded her of them, she would not have remembered them at all. Those were not the memories that came immediately to her mind; rather vignettes from her aloneness were what she easily recalled.

Lilly was a loner. She was comfortable keeping her own counsel. At a very early age she used fantasy, in addition to and at times in place of, socialization with family and others. This is probably why she learned to read at a very early age. Books open up wonderful worlds.

And Sean? I asked him if, in his leprechaun persona, he often visited retirement homes.

"Aye," he smiled. "I do those for free."

No surprise. His fondest, oldest memories are of endearing elderly people. He loves them to this day and goes out of his way for them. Also, his early memories always involved others. And he was hardly shy. Even when his behavior ostensibly embarrassed him, he enjoyed the attention he received. After all, asking food of a distant neighbor takes courage.

Sean is a people person. He enjoys others and their attention, both giving and receiving. He's open, friendly, and remarkably bold. He's always on the go. Just what you would expect of a leprechaun.

Lilly wagged her head sadly. "No wonder we have trouble. We're poles apart. How did we ever get together in the first place? We're incompatible."

Different, certainly. Incompatible? Certainly not.

It was my pleasure to lead them to an appreciation of each others' gifts. It was not by choice that they came together. "Falling in love" is directed by needs and wants far below the surface level of the mind. Each completed the other. Each provided what the other lacked. Well wedded, they formed a splendid team.

Several years ago we did a radio series on memories and their power, and the response to that series was phenomenal. In essence, that response spawned this book, for it revealed a strongly felt interest of our listeners. In that series Randy Carlson, coauthor of *Unlocking the Secrets of Your Childhood Memories*, turned the tables on Minirth Meier New Life Clinic psychotherapist Brian Newman and me. We were always analyzing other people; now we were to subject our earliest memories to his analysis.

Brian: "My earliest? I used to be an early riser. My parents had to put a lock on the *out*side of my door or little old Brian would be up and roaming the neighborhood. I would ride with the milkman to a cul-de-sac. There was one gentleman I used to go and wake up, and he'd sit on his porch with his coffee and give me a glass of milk, and we'd talk."

Randy: "What was the emotion?"

Brian: "Excitement. Pleasure and excitement."

Randy's analysis: Brian likes new and exciting things, different things. He's not afraid to step forth. He values relationships highly and is action oriented.

Randy was right on. How did he come to this conclusion? Little Brian was not afraid to go exploring and make himself a part of worlds not his own—the milkman's, for example, and the gentleman's in the cul-de-sac. He sought out companionship, a key to his present preferences. And in that very early remembrance, Brian was an active doer, not a passive observer.

I repeat that the emotional memories linger and are recorded in other areas of the memory as well. Brian still likes milk!

My turn: "I was about four, going horseback riding with Dad. No, I'd guess my earliest was my mother rocking me and rubbing my head. The emotions associated with both are wonderful. With Dad, fun. With Mom, comfort and security."

Randy's analysis: "Both memories are so active, not sedentary. Family is incredibly important; primary family members show up in both. This is a person who likes to have fun, be with others, likes to see things happen.

You see? The law of creative consistency. Millions of things happened to that little boy Frank Minirth, and out of them all, he remembers these.

3. Figure Out Yourself

Examine the elements of your own earliest memories.

Look for a key to your social preferences

Are you content alone or do you prefer company? Whose company? In the memory, are you alone or with others? Are family members prominent or neighbors or extended family? These are where your primary affections lay.

Look for a key to your temperament

Sean and Lilly learned that they are both actors, not reactors. They do things rather than passively await things to be done to them.

In your memory, are you active or passive? Are things done to you or are you influencing the situation?

Look for a key to your prevalent emotions

What were your feelings in the memory? What specifically triggered them? Was it your actions? Another's actions? Derision? Admiration?

Sean disregarded the soup lady's dirty looks in order to delight in the soup. His personality then was really quite a bit like his personality now. One of the reasons he was in his third marriage was because he threw caution to the wind in his pursuit of happiness and pleasure. Twice he married unwisely and both times, he decided in retrospect, for frivolous reasons.

To be honest he married Lilly for frivolous reasons. This time, though, he had a better understanding and admiration for his bride. He was going to stick it out and do whatever had to be done to make it work.

4. Understand Your Spouse

Sean and Lilly explored their earliest memories together. In fact, they helped each other analyze the memories. They both took care to accentuate the positive traits they uncovered. As I pointed out, with a child there is no such thing as positive or negative personality traits. Children adapt according to their God-given genetic tendencies. What we might call negative is, at that age, one of the options for surviving and coping. That's where parental shaping is so important.

If you are married, you would derive great benefit from performing this experiment as a couple. Help each other identify the basic motivations behind the child's actions or reactions. Ask the above questions and help each other answer them.

Next, explore these topics, individually, and as a couple:

- What is your view of life?
- How do the two of you differ? In what ways are you

similar? These are not necessarily points of conflict, although they may reveal sources of conflict.

- How can you help each other?

Sean figured this one out with no trouble. "When I'm about to leap into something boots and all, and often for little good reason, I need Lilly to pull me back and slap me around a bit to wake me up. She can help me resist this tendency in me."

That was an excellent insight. I pointed out, however, that it was not Lilly's responsibility to keep Sean out of trouble. Her responsibility ended with her warning. He was not in any way to blame her for troubles he might get into. It was still his life and his decisions. He was right; she could help. But she was not his mother or baby-sitter.

Sean could encourage the loner Lilly into better and deeper relationships with others. Her whole life she had essentially "gotten along without anyone else, thank you" to use her words. She had trouble relating well to others.

5. Identify Your Strengths and Weaknesses

Sean saw the trouble spots in his personality and, incidentally, also the strengths. His strengths far outweighed his weaknesses, but it was the weaknesses that got him into trouble.

Lilly's "weakness"—her difficulty forging and enjoying relationships—was not a problem as such. She was happy the way she was. She recognized, however, that her life would be much richer if she could get past her natural tendency and relate better to others. Also, she could enjoy a closer intimacy with Sean. So she used Sean's gregariousness to help her do that.

You will probably see, as Sean did, that a few elements of your personality are the cause of troubles and most elements are in fact very positive. Like Lilly, you may find places where your life could be richer and more satisfying if you weren't held back by the traits of that preschooler in your earliest memories.

You can do two things to change:

A. *Identify the traits you have and the traits you wish you had*

Identifying what you want to change is paramount, of course, because then you have a clear goal. Unless you know your destination, you are doomed to wander aimlessly and therefore fruitlessly.

B. *Behave and act the traits you wish*

You will find that behaving in new ways actually changes the way you think.

Sean would have to learn to consider choices more carefully, but he could do so. Lilly would have to learn to like people better, but she could do so. Both would be battling powerful forces—their memories. But as those forces changed, they could change their lives. You can alter your basic traits and habits. How?

Determination. What an amazing property of the human soul! It is the first of four final steps in the process that can actually change the way you think and respond.

6. *Make a Determination*

Right now, every moment, between 100,000 and 21,000,000 chemical reactions are occurring in your body. The exact number will depend upon whether you are working or thinking hard (or both!), when you've last eaten, and how cold it is around you. A very large proportion of those chemical reactions are happening in your brain.

That's a lot of power to focus on a project. It offers tremendous potential for change.

What about you? Has the exercise with the law of relative consistency shown you things you would like to change?

The initial step, to determine what to change, is very simple and very profound. First Sean and Lilly pledged, "From now on I am going to change [such-and-so] pattern of thinking by changing my behavior. I am going to reprogram for improvement." That is the determination.

Sean and Lilly made an additional statement, a joint commitment to improve through the manipulation of memory and to help each other's efforts. Going into this process with a buddy or support group is always very helpful.

What would your determination be? Frame it as a single sentence. Write it down. Rewrite the sentence.

If absolutely necessary give yourself a compromise rather than an all-out promise. For example, Lilly would, for starters, set limits on the amount of socializing she would force herself to do when she joined a group of some sort. She made that promise to herself so that she could keep her determination more easily.

7. Decide on Actions

How would a person behave if the desired change was already in place? Sean would curb impulsive and frivolous decisions, Lilly would "mix" more with other people.

How would you behave if your desired change were complete?

Notice that no one said anything about new thoughts to fit

the determination. You cannot shortcut the process and say, "I determine to change the way I think about [such-and-so]." Won't work. Thinking and acting are both based on accumulated memory, and accumulated memory is too strong and too far-flung within your brain to change easily. This is one of several reasons (the others being physiological in nature) that women on diets lose weight but usually fail to keep the lost pounds off. It is that accumulated memory we are going to work on. The new ways of thinking will follow.

Call our conscious self "the upper brain" and make "the lower brain" the realm of thinking and memory that works below conscious level. Another way of saying it: the upper is voluntary, the lower involuntary. We already know how profoundly the lower levels of thinking affect the upper levels. Over 80 percent of every *rational* decision you make is made in the lower brain. However, the upper brain can leverage just as much influence upon the lower brain in different ways. We will use this concept to change the lower brain.

Also, the body does what the brain wants it to. However, the converse is true as well. The brain does what the body wants it to, if the body insists hard enough. We will walk in both directions on this two-way street in order to reprogram.

When a situation comes up which requires the new you to behave differently than the old you would, you pause long enough to actively think.

8. Recognize New Responses

Say to yourself, *Based upon the new choices I'm making, this is how I ought to respond to this situation.*

And the next-to-the-last step is like unto it:

9. Perform the New Actions

Lilly said skeptically, "That sounds too easy to be workable."

Not easy, exactly, but possible. Certainly workable. As you change your behavior consistently, the memories follow suit.

When babies are happy, they clap their hands (or try to; coordination sometimes lags in this area). It's programmed in. To make babies happy, physically (and gently!) pat those tiny hands together. Laugh and smile as you do it. The babies get right with the program. Now I admit that when babies are hungry or frightened or angry, no amount of clapping is going to work for long. But you see the general principle. If the body goes through the actions consistently, the mind follows.

Current research is proving this more and more. One of the major ways to get people to change is simply to get them acting in the new way. You can use this principle.

"No," Lilly said. "I can see when it's plain old behavior. But when strong emotions are involved . . . no. I can't stop myself fast enough to control them."

Right. No one can. Let me cite the example of a woman we will call Jolene. Jolene could sense anger in others a mile away, an ability that in itself is not a bad thing. But feelings of anger or displeasure in others instantly triggered her anger. Her initial reaction was invariably, "It's unjust to be angry with me!" regardless of the perceived reason. To say she was overly sensitive is an understatement. Any perceived displeasure on their part made her furious.

However, she determined to change. "When I feel a hostile reaction on another person's part, I will stop instantly and tell myself to act friendly anyway."

Notice that she said *act friendly*, not *feel friendly*.

A few hours after she made that pledge, Jolene got the chance to exercise it. She stopped to get the paper and called "good morning" to her neighbor. The neighbor, scowling, walked off. Jolene's first reaction was to run back in the house and mark the neighbor off her Christmas card list. But she wanted to change her behavior. She stopped.

Jolene thought that she would not be so sensitive if she saw the world, as well as herself, more clearly from others' viewpoints. So Jolene determined to try to ascertain that viewpoint.

She was furious, but she was determined not to let her fury rule her. So she ran to catch up to the neighbor and kept her voice pleasant. "Good morning. You seem upset with me. Is something wrong?"

"Yes," fumed the neighbor, and pointed to Jolene's cocker spaniel, Taffy, exploring the neighbor's hedge. "I'm getting pretty tired of cleaning up after your dog every morning."

"I'll try not to let it happen again," Jolene said. "Thank you for letting me know."

They parted.

Jolene was absolutely irate. Her dog didn't do that *that* much! Certainly not *every* morning. And she couldn't control where Taffy went.

Jolene had pledged that every time she sensed anger in another person, whether it was real or not, she would try to trade viewpoints with the other person. She was regretting that promise.

But she bought a thirty-foot leash and put it on Taffy every morning when she sent him out. Jolene was not the only one whose behavior was going to be modified.

To Jolene's amazement, within the next few weeks just about everyone on the block started being cheerier.

What about Lilly and Sean? Let's say Lilly is invited to one of the parties Sean is going to work. *No thanks*, she thinks. She stops. Thinks again. She won't enjoy herself if she goes. She hates those mingle-mingle-mingle too-much-drinking affairs. But she's determined to change her behavior. She decides to go and mingle with no more than two persons. That's a manageable compromise to not going at all.

So she tags along with Sean and tries not to act reluctant. That's a part of it, you see. She must act enjoyment as well as think enjoyment. Make the body do what the mind is supposed to pick up on.

Actually, it's kind of neat—and certainly unique—to arrive at a party on the arm of a leprechaun. As Sean works the crowd, producing gold doubloons out of thin air and from behind people's ears, Lilly watches with great pleasure. She's never seen him in full performance.

She strikes up a conversation with a quiet woman in a corner. Sean told her in advance that if she wanted to meet the more reticent party goers, head for the corners. The woman is a writer who creates advertising brochures for a computer firm. On the side she writes murder mysteries but has yet to get one published. Lilly loves to read. They spend half an hour chatting about books.

In his supportive role, Sean minimizes Lilly's party experience by taking her home early, as soon as his duties are completed. Out the door and in the car, she is astonished to realize that she was reluctant to go.

Notice that these three people did not pledge a breezy "I'm going to change my whole outlook!" No, they made small, incremental pledges, one definite step at a time. Lilly pledged to talk to two people. That's all. She ended up arranging to have lunch with one of them, the writer, having struck up a delightful acquaintance. So she was ready to move beyond her pledge, but she made the original promise modest enough to be workable.

When Jolene pledged to try to see each situation from someone else's viewpoint, she did not pledge to adopt that viewpoint. She certainly did not pledge to avoid becoming angry. That would have been beyond her because it's an automatic reaction. She kept her goals focused and limited.

So ought you. Make a determination. Decide on an action that would promote the determination. Act on it. Repeat the actions as much as possible. I assure you, you will grow.

Think how often you have heard someone say, "He's not the man I married twenty years ago."

"She's different now, more certain of herself. I guess it's the social and political climate or something."

What it is, is growth. Men and women are changed by the consistent input of new material. That's what growing is. The final stage, then, is a continuing process rather than a single shot.

10. Do It Over and Over

Repetition is what makes memories permanent. We looked at that earlier as a reason so many memories are deeply ingrained. Now we're looking at it from the other side. If you want to engrain a memory deeply, repeat it.

We remember what we repeat. What we do not repeat tends to be forgotten, in that we lose the retrieval triggers. In a sense we tend to lose what we program over.

Now be advised that in extremity—when a sudden emergency nails you—you are likely to revert to your earliest ways of doing things. The little child's attitudes will be the first to influence your actions. That is especially true of remembered emotions, even emotions apart from the memory of the incidents that spawned them. A similar situation today will trigger the original feelings. Understanding that this is what is happening will alleviate the problem to a degree. Changing behavior will repair it. The little child's reactions will fade as your redirected attitudes and traits gain strength. You will remember you have grown.

In this chapter we've been looking at the memories that form our personalities. In part two we will look specifically at bad memories. Do bad memories occur only in a sexual connotation? Of course not. Those kinds of experiences receive a great deal of attention, but they are a minority of bad memories. The great majority are small, irritating, and at times, disabling ones. Everyone has them. And after all, on a day to day basis, it's not the problem of world hunger that rubs us, it's coat hangers tangled up in the closet.

At their worst, bad memories affect our health in serious ways. Let's look next at bad memories.

WHEN MEMORY WORKS AGAINST US

5

Can Our Memories Be Distorted?

I t's today's headlines. Even as children tell harrowing stories of abuse, defenders for the accused show how those children's memories could easily have been invented. A woman comes forward many years after the fact to describe how her father murdered a nine-year-old playmate. The Rodney King videotape has been played over and over so many times it has become something of a national memory, forged in the minds of millions of people who have never been to Los Angeles. Everybody, it seems, is messing with everybody else's mind.

Whether memories can be altered, whether they are untrue, and to what extent this all takes place have become important legal issues. I do not intend to get into legal issues here. But any person wrestling with memories, particularly bad memories, wants to know how far memories can be trusted. Can they be invented? Can some sinister force change them without the recaller's knowledge? Can people make up memories? These are important considerations.

A woman named Genevieve tells this interesting story. "My husband on several occasions has described, in my presence, the time he saw a UFO. It was a white dot the same brightness as a first magnitude star. It was moving across the night sky at a solid, steady rate, about due northwest. He pointed to it and said, 'There goes a satellite.' Then, without changing speed in any way, it suddenly hung a ninety-degree sharply-angled left turn and continued as it had been, straight arc line, southwest. No satellite turns abruptly like that at a sharp right angle; no airplane, either.

"Now here's the really weird part. My husband claims that he had our son with him the night he saw it, not me, and that he came home and told me about it. I think I was the person with him. I remember that sight so vividly, the white dot cutting a right angle in the sky. But I can't think why I would have been with him. Did I see it, or did his description paint such a perfect picture that my mind adopted it as an actual memory?"

Can memories, in other words, be invented?

Are the Memories You Have Accurate?

If Genevieve's memory was indeed created whole, the conditions were right. The event occurred late at night, and people are most susceptible to suggestion when they are weary, hungry, worn down, or ill. (Young people are even more susceptible than adults.) It was a very simple image cast literally in black and white—a dot against the starry night sky. Simplest reproduces best. And it was startling. Even if you could invent a memory of something bland and innocuous—say, canned peaches—what would be the point? The startling, the exciting, the unexpected are more likely to be emblazoned on memory.

Can memories be invented or distorted? Yes. If conditions are right; if the description is vivid enough, and especially if it addresses more than one sense (taste plus vision, perhaps, or smell plus sound); if the desire to remember a described thing is strong enough, the mind can adopt as its own a memory that has been created elsewhere. But that is exceedingly rare. More often, an existing memory, or perhaps a very similar memory, is altered to fit the described occasion.

Alterations occur by both addition and subtraction.

Adding to Memories

Expanding upon memories is actually not all that uncommon. Our brain does it a lot. In a highly publicized day-care center molestation case, the children's stories shifted nebulously. Facts were added. Some changed. I'm not going to get into the legal ramifications, but this is a normal function of memory, especially with growing children. It causes havoc in court cases, but it occurs naturally and for good reason.

Children are not the only ones whose memories are subject to manipulation. As an experiment in memory, a professor brought a group of students into his office and asked them to look around very carefully. He then sent them out into the next room and instructed them to write down everything they had noticed in the office. They were to list only those things they were absolutely certain they had seen. Every single one of them mentioned books.

There were no books in the office. Not one.

Those students' minds, like yours, constantly play an instantaneous game of mix and match. The students saw the office. They knew books were supposed to be there, reference books especially. The office wouldn't be complete without reference books.

Think of any office. In my own office a bookcase beside my desk contains over 150 volumes. That's the small one. Two of the walls are nothing but bookshelves, all crammed. And I believe my office is typical. The brain of every student who took part in the experiment matched what was seen against what it "knew" ought to be and deduced below conscious level that books ought to be there. And so every person "saw" them.

Their brains literally inserted the missing books into their memories so that the scene would be correct and complete.

The memory takes the swiftly passing scene that our senses provide and literally fills in the blanks. It's like making a quick line sketch of a moving horse, then filling in the details and shading later. If you know a lot about horse anatomy and you draw horses well, the final drawing will be lifelike and convincing. Your brain strives to keep all its memories totally lifelike and convincing. This often requires additions after the fact.

A very small child would not put books on a list of things in that professor's office because a child would have no conviction that books ought to be there. As children grow, their memories grow. Young memories are reprocessed according to their new outlook on life. We will go into this in detail in chapter six. A child called to the witness stand two years after the remembered incident is not at all the child who first experienced the incident. Children change drastically and their memories and perceptions change along with them. Their memories expand and fill in, in part, but not completely, to fit their new maturity.

Even the children can sense the changes within them. A child terrified of the monster under the bed at age four cannot, at age seven, imagine what was so scary about an imaginary beast.

Where does the mind get the fill-in material? Mostly, your memory fills in the blanks with what it already "knows." Let's say that an experienced bird-watcher sees a tiny black-capped bird fly by. The bird-watcher happens to know that in this particular region he can expect either chestnut-backed chickadees or mountain chickadees. He doesn't glimpse the white eye stripe that sets apart mountain chickadees from all other tiny black-capped birds. So even though he doesn't really see the bird's back, either, he "sees" the reddish brown color. His mind filled that in because it ought to be there. Were that a drastically out-of-range Carolina chickadee flying by, the seasoned bird-watcher would quite possibly miss the true identification. He wasn't expecting it, and his mind "saw" something else.

Subtracting from Memories

Memories fade with time. They disappear completely if the neurons carrying them die. Details that are lost or faded might remain lost, or they might be reconstructed in the same way additions are made. Generally speaking, if that occurs, you cannot tell the new patch from the old cloth.

Memory and mood feed upon each other. The person in a sour mood when an incident occurs is going to remember the negative elements of that incident more so than the positive ones. The person will in essence subtract the cheerful aspects. Conversely, people who are happy at the time of the event take a more positive outlook toward it. Also, positive emotions do more than negative emotions toward facilitating memory. So your mood may well subtract things from time to time.

This subtraction can cause problems. If you happen to be in the throes of a depression, your whole memory bank is adversely affected. "Happy event? What happy event? Nothing happy ever happens to me."

The biggest subtraction comes through denial. Whole memories and major segments of lives might be subtracted. This is becoming more obvious as we delve into the horrors of sexual abuse, especially incest. In fact, sexual interference is the major area in which the validity of memory is most severely tested, in legal as well as medical circles.

In her book, *Secret Survivors*, E. Sue Blume lists the aftereffects of abuse that she looks for in counsel. These are some of them:

- Night terrors
- A blatant disregard for health and for one's own body, ignoring such common health practices as going to the doctor (The person will also engage in

behavior that can cause personal injury—anything from recklessness to smoking.)

- Fear or repulsion at being touched
- A history of sexual acting out, such as promiscuity or freezing up; a pattern of relationships with older or more powerful partners; no sexual enjoyment
- Difficulty with water hitting the face (How well does the person tolerate showers rather than baths and walking in the rain?)
- An exaggerated or overly sensitive gag reflex
- Inappropriate clothing (too sexy or not sexy enough, i.e. baggy, overly concealing); covering the neck, perhaps always wearing turtlenecks
- Discomfort using public bathrooms

Blume works primarily with women, but men are abuse victims also, particularly when we're talking about childhood abuse. (This is not a book on abuse issues. If you see these traits in yourself or a loved one, investigate further.)

Denial not only erases memories, it reduces them.

Over and over, women who have been abused incestuously will report that "Dad" or "Uncle" or "Brother" or whoever "did it once." Actually, almost no incest is limited to one occasion unless the perpetrator is physically removed from contact (as by moving away or dying). Incest commonly occurs as numerous incidents. And yet, the victims will often remember only one.

Rearranging Elements of Memories

I remember hearing a story concerning an incident in the county courthouse of a small town. A man was brought to trial for murder. Three witnesses took the stand and positively identified him as the culprit. Suddenly a sheriff's deputy, very much agitated, entered and begged a recess. He had made a drastic error. He had sent the wrong man over from the jail. The accused murderer was still incarcerated. The fellow who had just been positively identified as a murderer by three citizens was actually slated for a later trial on auto theft charges. In fact, at the time of the murder he was a hundred miles away serving a prison term for an unrelated offense.

Those three witnesses were certainly not trying to railroad an innocent man. They carried the courage of their convictions. But memories can lie. They can play tricks. They can change.

In that incident the witnesses' brains played another sort of trick. I've mentioned the way your brain will sift through memories of similar incidents in order to know how to handle a new situation. The witnesses' brains did something like that. Here was the man identified by the prosecutor as the murderer. He looked more or less like the perpetrator they had seen (actually, less; it was not a close resemblance). Their brains made the connection of perpetrator with perpetrator and mistakenly—but in all honesty—believed that connection was factual.

You must be careful, therefore, about giving extreme credence to any detail of memories. That includes, incidentally, photographic memories. Even the amazing fellow who can read a stockholders' report once and then quote every figure in it, plus the page numbers, must not trust his memory completely in the long term. He too is constantly constructing and reconstructing his memories.

This is a blessing. If memories are not chiseled in stone, we can work with them in positive ways. So rejoice that your mind is constantly fiddling with them. You can use that attribute for making positive changes in your life.

It sounds then like memory is not accurate and you shouldn't trust the pictures and stories from your past. On the contrary. You would be amazed at how accurate those records are!

Trusting Possibly-Altered Memories

"The first time it happened, I thought it was just one of those little freaks your mind pulls sometimes. I thought it was a blip in my radar. Then it happened again and then again, and I thought I was going crazy." A young woman we will call Sue was talking about weird flashbacks. At the time they began occurring, she did not know what flashbacks were. She found out.

"While my husband and I were making love, I suddenly had this very real impression of hair in my face. Real! It was stiff, curly, almost wiry hair, and it was literally stuffed up against my face. And sweaty. I freaked. My husband is not hairy-chested. His chest is very smooth, in fact. And he certainly wasn't sweaty. The impression only lasted a few moments and then it passed, but by then I was flipped. The poor man didn't know what was wrong, of course. Neither did I.

"Two weeks later it happened again. And when it happened a third time, he insisted I get help to find out what's going on. So here I am. What is my imagination doing to me, Doctor?"

Sue's imagination was doing nothing to her, but her memories were.

Figment or Fact?

Her first question was one so many people ask. "Am I making it up out of my imagination, or did it really happen?" Sometimes the answer is hard to determine.

People who are experiencing bad memories, of course, are hoping their heads are just making it up. If the memories are not being constructed of whole cloth, the alternative is, "I am going to have to deal with some nasty stuff." That's never a comforting thought.

But it's not just a mental game. Bad memories that are real have what we call a quality of discovery. People who make up things also remember the process of making them up. In other words you're not discovering a memory, you're inventing it, and you know you're inventing it, and you remember inventing it. When that memory of inventing a memory does not exist, chances are good the memory is real. It is a discovered thing rather than a created thing.

Frequently with a bad memory, you can ask yourself the rhetorical question, "Who in his right mind would make up something like that?" Sue certainly would not deliberately, or even subconsciously, invent a memory of hair pressed against her face.

The best answer to *Is it real?* though, doesn't actually fit the question, and it's not nearly as rewarding as a simple yes or no. The best answer is, *It doesn't matter.* Now of course this is not satisfying in a legal context, particularly as regards sexual interference and abuse. But the victim, or purported victim if you wish, still has to work through it, whether or not it's truth. A persistent flashback or bad memory casts thoughts and feelings into disarray. Flashbacks are especially telling because they indicate something deep down inside needs attention fast. It's festering. Even if it's fictitious, you have to do something about it.

Proceed with Caution

I suggest as a rule of thumb you treat unwelcome memories and flashbacks as being accurate, or fairly so. If they are accurate, you must deal with them. If they are not, they represent some powerful forces at work below the conscious level. And those forces, whatever they are, must be addressed or they will continually cause problems.

If Sue's problem was investigated and treated in a hospital setting, three weeks of work in the hospital would equal about seven months of outpatient care and attention. In the hospital setting patients get several hours of intensive work every day.

When people first walk in the hospital, we let them know that a week from now they will feel even worse than they do presently. "It really hurts for a while," we tell them, "as you wade through the garbage that is clamoring for attention. You've got to get through it until eventually, relief, peace, wholesome love, and joy come. And come they will."

Sue's case is significant in another important respect. She started working on her problem in an office counseling environment, then began to feel desperate and terrified, and moved into a hospital environment. Wise decision. If you notice at any time that your memories and your feelings are getting out of control, perhaps even rampaging, get the level of help you need. That may mean a counselor's attention, a crisis worker's attention, or hospitalization. Whatever. Just don't delay.

The problem we uncovered with Sue was early childhood molestation. The flashback experience eventually took more recognizable form as a memory of her stepfather. He was a hairy-chested man.

Any sexual interference in childhood is highly intrusive. You *must* be extremely gentle and cautious in dealing with it. There is the memory itself of violation, of helplessness, of a severe loss of trust. Imagine your life if there is no safety net to protect you from violation. Then there is the secondary message such interference spells out, and believe me, a small child instinctively understands it: "Your needs and wishes are not important. Mine are." This implication about the child's self-worth is extremely strong and extremely penetrating at all levels of memory. It sticks like glue forever after.

It stuck in Sue until the festering was so great that her mind rebelled and produced the flashbacks.

Yes, But Dreams Aren't Real, Are They?

Dreams are expected to be wildly weird. You fly like Tinkerbell, breathe underwater, fall incredible distances, do all sorts of unreal things. The strangeness is merely your brain at work. At times our unconscious thoughts and fears come up in dreams. These include things we are afraid of and wishes we would like to see fulfilled. Irritations crop up in dreams. Sometimes when stress makes life a little heavy, dreams will reflect the things we are worrying about at the moment. Dreams, then, are one of the ways we process the odd elements of life.

Dreams are very real in the sense they reflect real issues within the mind. The situations may be absurd, but the underlying themes are what you consider. The themes—fears, ugly situations, confusing scenes—will reflect problems that must be handled.

If you are going to examine your dreams, write them down instantly, the moment you awaken. They are not meant to stay with you, and they will evaporate rapidly. If you want to hang on to anything at all, write as fast as you can.

As you examine your dreams, then, look for consistent underlying themes, the same basic message in a variety of weird venues. Constantly dreaming about certain things will many times show you how your mind is dealing with specific issues. Recurring themes and dreams suggest a knotty problem not being resolved. Scattered themes may just be the pizza and soda you had for dinner.

Psychotherapist Brian Newman relates the story of a woman he worked with several years ago. Suddenly, apparently without provocation, the woman began experiencing anew the bad memories she thought had been resolved. Now here they were, coming up in a new way. They were riddling her dreams, night after night.

If that sort of thing occurs with you, we suggest you get into a support group that understands or possibly meet with a therapist or pastor. In any circumstance, pray for the wisdom to know what to do with your unwanted dreams or memories. Believe it, Satan uses our own memories to defeat us. And that is sad, because it is unnecessary. Help is out there.

Before you tackle any task, particularly any difficult task, your first course of action is to pray for wisdom as you go, especially the wisdom of God. You must also decide what sort of help to seek.

As I mentioned earlier, bad memories affect our health in serious ways. Let's look next at the ways that memory works against us.

6

Unhappy Memories—All of Us Have Some

Gretchen's father always insisted that suffering builds character, and he wanted Gretchen to have lots of character. "I grew up in the Depression," he was fond of saying. "We suffered then. We had to make do. Kids today don't suffer enough. They have it too easy, which is why they're such soft, whining fops. I don't want you being any soft, whining fop, Gretch."

"Yes, Dad."

"Look at me! Character!"

"You sure are, Dad."

Gretchen's dad and mom had worked throughout their childhood, helping their families survive. Now, despite the fact that they were well off and survival was no longer an issue, it was Gretchen's turn to work. From the age of six on, she carried a heavy load of housework along with schoolwork. Her father arranged an outside job for her the minute she could get a work permit. Her earnings went into the family bank account. On the family's frequent camping trips, she pitched the tent, hauled the water, built the fires, washed the pots and pans. Her father liked to think of camping as recreation. She remembered it as hard work.

Now Gretchen sat in my office, literally burned out at the age of forty-seven. She chain-smoked, suffered a prescription drug dependency, and had just been caught shoplifting in a major department store.

She grimaced. "He built my character, all right. Look at me. A druggie who steals. Dr. Minirth, I have enough money. Not wealthy, but very comfortable. I didn't need that scarf. I didn't even really want that scarf. I can't imagine why I took it."

"Did you simply forget to pay as you left?"

"No, it was deliberate. I have to admit it. It was absolutely, totally stupid, but deliberate. And I have no idea why I did it. No idea. Doctor, am I going crazy?"

It was my pleasure to assure her in that very first session that she certainly was not going insane. She was actually behaving normally, although not in a very laudible way at times, and she possessed a strong, even noble, character. She had been trapped by her past and imprisoned by her memories. Over the next six months we sifted through those memories. No, we could not change her father's actions or her recent behavior. But we turned the memories of them around to her benefit.

Think for a moment about your worst memories. What happened that you wish never had? Would you change some of that if you could? Of course you would!

"You can't change the past! It happened. It's done," my patients tell me. And it's true. But that doesn't mean you are imprisoned by it. As we explore bad memories in greater detail we will develop ways to turn them to good use. Your worst memories can make you a happier, more productive servant of God. They really can!

Let me offer a word of warning that I will repeat more than once. To illustrate, a lady was listening to our radio series, she told us, when her life became so heavy with old memories surfacing that she had to turn off the radio and regroup. She did exactly the right thing. This book may trigger memories in you that can lead to painful recall, even panic or anxiety. If this occurs *immediately* call someone and tell the person what is happening. Don't face such a powerful force as your memory alone if trouble threatens. Let someone help you take care of it.

Gretchen's bad memories were not terrible images of deliberate, easily-identifiable abuse. She wasn't abused sexually or physically. They were images of relentless parental control and work, work, work. Even that was not all bad. Her father really did have the best of intentions. Besides, she took a personal pride in her work. She was good at it. She enjoyed some of the jobs she held.

Along with bad memories, Gretchen had the problem of no memories. This was not, like Glenn or Kevin whom we've met, parts of her life blanked out. She simply never had time to play. She was robbed of her childhood. When her friends were out enjoying each other and, even more importantly, learning through trial and error how to interact at a deep personal level, she was working as a busser and waitress, interacting with strangers at a very superficial level. She never married because she could develop no deep or lasting attachments.

Gretchen had to tackle two problems. One was her inability to form satisfying emotional attachments to people. The other was her penchant for passive self-destruction. She presents an interesting question that you also may have to answer. "How much of a possibly sordid past do I *have* to remember for my own good?" How far do you push it? Do you dig or simply let sleeping dogs lie?

How to Decide If You Should Tackle Bad Memories

Ron Houser, who couldn't remember large blocks of his childhood, shrugged it off. It was his wife who insisted they investigate the weirdness. An apparent absence of memories can be classed as "bad memories" if they are in fact suppressed.

On the other hand, Gretchen's answer was, "Start digging." Her problems were messing up her life. That answer may not be appropriate for you. If you wonder if you should look into your bad memories (or even wonder if you have some you're not aware of), ask yourself these questions:

Do You Have Poor Health?

You've seen lists of the physical ailments that arise because of stress. Migraine and tension headaches loom large. Intestinal disorders such as colitis and ulcers occur. Heart problems can arise, as can such neurological symptoms as tics and extreme muscle aches and tension. These are a few of the possible problems.

Everything that plain, unadorned stress can cause can also be caused by the irritation of bad, painful memories. Bad memories often generate guilt or anger, bringing on the above problems secondarily. If your health is shaky or if you suffer chronic problems, your memories may need to be mended.

Do You Have Flashbacks and Bad Dreams?

"What's a flashback, exactly?" Gretchen asked.

A flashback is a moment of vivid, intrusive memory that comes and then is gone. It can occur in a dream or when you are awake. It often pops in and out during an intense moment while you are deeply involved in something else. For example, women who were raped or subjected to incest might experience a flashback during sexual activity many years later, as Sue did. It can take the form of a mere smell, a vague sensation, a sound, or a complete memory vignette.

Some persons report image flashbacks in which they see only an isolated something. An example is Rita, subjected to incest at the age of eight. To avoid thinking about what was happening to her, she focused all her attention on a yellow picture frame beside her bed. Denial blocked out her memory of the abuse itself. The picture frame began recurring as a flashback twenty years later. Flashbacks generally take the form of intrusive thoughts and images that have no immediate relevance to whatever you are doing or thinking at the moment.

The dreams will fit a recognizable pattern if you think about them. Such clues say that your brain's program is on overload. The memories keep intruding.

Random nightmares and other such phenomena are merely the brain working out its problems and fears. If you analyze nightmares and strange dreams, you will probably notice that they reflect a weird, twisted variation of something new that has been going on in your life lately. For example, a friend of mine described her terrifying dreams of volcanoes that occurred just before she transferred to a clinic in the Northwest. This was two months after Mount St. Helens erupted. Her conscious mind knew there was absolutely no real danger in moving to Seattle, but her mind below conscious level had to work it out.

Most bad dreams are easy to figure out, and they quit happening in a matter of weeks. However, if the same theme or the same dream, keeps recurring, pay attention. Your brain is not simply working through the matter. Apparently the matter will not be resolved. The recurrent theme or dream then is worth considering as a clue to something trying to push up from below.

Flashbacks and dreams that exist as mere annoyances may or may not be a sign you should seek help. How annoying are they? You weigh the prospects of relief against the cost of getting that relief. But if these intrusions interfere at all with your work, your spiritual life, or your personal relationships, by all means start the healing process.

Are You Functioning Poorly?

If you are doing well socially and you are getting along well in your job, let it go. Delving into bad memories is properly an interest for people like Gretchen who are having trouble in their relationships with other people.

A seventy-year-old man described a lot of passive abuse in his early days, vivid recollections of neglect and ugliness. Then he asked, "Should I be doing something about those memories? My kids say I ought to. Two of them are in therapy, and they say they feel so much better."

Not only had he accomplished much in his life, he was still doing so when I spoke with him. Active in a square dance club, a carving group, and a choir, he hadn't slowed down a bit. I told him, "Don't bother. You're doing fine."

Maladaptive behavior—a fancy way of saying you are repeatedly messing up your life—is another sign. Ron Houser could be called a fairly typical example. He wanted to act responsibly, but he repeatedly acted without a shred of thought about consequences or the future. Too often he acted in ways that made him hate himself. That was maladaptive behavior, constant thoughts and actions that literally endangered him and whittled down his self-esteem.

Any behavior taken to excess can be maladaptive. It doesn't have to be immoral or even wrong. It's something you don't stop because you cannot stop, and anyway, you don't want to. Working, working, working can be damaging when your work destroys your personal relationships. Affair, affair, affair. Paranoia. One groundless suspicion after another. You find yourself in a wild, blind search for some elusive quality, and your actions simply are not getting you any satisfaction for your hunger.

I recall the case of a movie actress who had married five alcoholics. She was batting a thousand, but it was certainly maladaptive. Together we uncovered that her father had molested her and abused her. Way down deep, she thought she desperately needed to help her father and punish herself for all the false guilt her disastrous childhood generated. So, she married men who needed help, surrogate fathers, and punished herself very effectively in the process.

When I told her this, she stormed out. Ten days later she returned somewhat sheepishly and gave me 147 handwritten pages journaling the memories that had erupted during that intervening week. I had been right on. Then we sat down and went to work on the healing.

Another problem of function involves psychosomatic illness. Here is one of the areas in which memory problems fall directly over into the realm of physical health. The word *psychosomatic* is so terribly misunderstood. "It's all in your head," the unsympathetic advisor will say. Certainly there is a mental element, the *psycho* part of the word reflects that. But *somatic* refers to the body, and the illness is very real, very physical. It is not imagined. It is there. You can die just as quickly from the heart attack caused by repressed memories as from the heart attack caused by high cholesterol.

Psychosomatic (a word coined by a Christian psychiatrist over a hundred years ago) illnesses have a foundation in stress, anxiety, fear, and worry. These mental conditions trigger physiological responses, which in turn cause physical signs and symptoms. Paul Meier pointed out in our radio series that 80 percent of medical problems are based in some underlying emotional problem rather than having a purely physical cause.

Colitis, labile hypertension (that is, blood pressure that soars and dips unpredictably), peptic ulcers, migraines, and other headaches are some possible illnesses that can indicate repression. Your mind, not wanting to look at certain memories, may be finding it easier and less painful to displace the real worry and concern with something physical.

If a person can't function well, he or she has a problem. If the person can't function at all, and that sometimes happens, he or she has a *real* problem that will only get worse if neglected.

Are You Plagued by Emotional Difficulties?

"Irritable?" Gretchen asked. "Ask my boyfriend. He'll call me up and talk to me a few minutes. I recently found out that what he's doing is listening to my tone of voice. If he hears my irritability and depression coming through, he backs off. He just flat out refuses to associate with me until I sweeten up. I ought to dump him."

Persistent anxiety, excessive nervousness, irritability, and depression are all clues that memories have an unwholesome influence on your life.

Anxiety is a feeling of fearfulness when there's no clear object to be afraid of. It's fear without focus. Elaine Houser would sometimes feel panicky. She would break out in a cold sweat. She'd feel terrified and had no idea what she felt terrified about. Anxiety can occur in a less vivid form with similar but milder symptoms, or it can nail you with feelings far more intense than Elaine's. Often it can also be a fear of knowing the truth, which means truth is buried somewhere. I have found that once truth is brought to the surface and resolved, the anxiety disappears.

Everyone suffers from depression now and then. But we look for distressing symptoms that render an individual nonfunctional without the person knowing why. For example, a teenager, notorious for ups and downs, goes into a deep and lengthy depression over a bad grade in biology. Anger, yes. Depression for a short while, maybe, if the grade really meant a lot. But "deep and lengthy" is an overreaction. It's a sign that something else is going on.

Agoraphobia can really cripple a person. This is the fear of leaving the house, a fear of crowds, a terror of driving on freeways. Whatever the condition, if it keeps you from doing well in your home, work, or school world, it is worth looking at very closely.

Do You See Overly Strong Defense Mechanisms?

"Like what?" Ron asked.

"How about *displacement?*" I asked.

Displacement is when you have a bad day at work, so you go home and kick the dog. It's when you overreact to your spouse or someone else close, blowing up for scant reason. It's when, because you happen to have bad memories toward a stepfather or someone, you can't stand any of the men in your life.

You also displace your anger at God. Of course, if you knew the truth of the situation, and also knew the reality of God, you wouldn't be mad at Him. You couldn't be. So that's displacement too.

"I do have one little problem others have told me about," Ron said. "*Projection.* I can't stand tardiness, but I'm almost always late for some reason I can't control. That's projection, right?"

Right. When you find some minor issue intolerable in someone else and it turns out you have the same problem, that's projection.

A really tricky defense mechanism to pick up on is *introjection.* You feel overly guilty for something you've done.

Elaine gasped, wide-eyed. "Oh, that's me! You don't know how guilty I feel sometimes. I can feel guilty just for existing. I'm not kidding. I thought it was just a nasty little quirk in me, and then I feel guilty about feeling guilty so much."

It's all my fault. That's just another way of expressing introjection. When a person feels rejected, one way to feel important again is to assume the guilt. "If it's all my fault," the unconscious self reasons, "that puts me at the center. I make things happen, even if they're terrible things."

These guilt-ridden folks are the people, incidentally, who do great rescue work—pastors, counselors, paramedics, search-

and-rescue people. Dandy fixer-uppers, they're out to fix the problem.

Another unexpected way in which defense kicks in is *control*. Everyone wants to be in control. That's normal. But are you overly controlling and rigid when you don't have to be? That's what we look for. One way people try to hide the past and ease the insecurity the past wrought in them is to keep a tight grip on life. It's strictly a surface defense. So long as they maintain tight control, they believe, the more secure and less vulnerable they will be.

But it doesn't work that way. The only thing rigid control produces is more rigid control. Too, the more abused a person is in childhood, the more perfectionistic and controlling he or she will be in adulthood.

As I mentioned, everyone has these defense mechanisms to some degree. They are the bumpers that keep our ship of life from scraping against the pier too badly. It's how we all get through life. When we're looking for evidence of repressed memories, we look for the overuse and abuse of these mechanisms.

Elaine looked suspicious. "I suppose this is all scriptural as well."

"Try Matthew 7:3–5," I said.

"That's the passage about a speck in your brother's eye when there's a plank in your own eye," she said. "That's hypocrisy."

"It's also projection."

Are You Tempted to Do Something That Is Legally or Morally Wrong?

Here was another biggie in Gretchen's life. She knew right from wrong, and she broke the law in spite of herself. Something big and ugly was happening, and it behooved her to get to the bottom of it. Do you see major flaws in your character that keep surfacing? Examples are an interest in unwholesome things such as pornography, an extramarital affair or a desire for one, shoplifting or pilferage, excessive drinking, gambling, serious obsessions and compulsions.

"That's deliberate criminal behavior," some would say. "You are condoning criminal behavior. Excusing it."

And I would respond, "Not at all. Gretchen didn't want to behave that way. She had no idea why she did such a thing. Getting to the bottom of her behavior and fixing it is not condoning the action. It's correcting the action."

If symptoms such as the above aren't there, or seem minimal, don't worry about it. If a situation comes up that appears to exceed what is natural for the average person, then deal with it. However, always keep in mind that everyone possesses a share of bad memories. That's life. In fact, as we will discuss later, trying to prevent bad memories is worse than having them. But if you answered yes to a couple of the symptoms, then you might want to talk to a counselor or minister.

Understand the Types of Bad Memories

Different people categorize negative memories in all sorts of ways. About the best of the systems is David Seamands's four H's: hurts, humiliations, horrors, and hates. All four can be minimized, but essentially you cannot avoid them 100 percent of the time. In other words, everyone has some. They are all four particularly potent when they strike small children.

Hurts

Hurts can be physical, when one person strikes or harms another. More often, though, they leave no surface scars. Emotional abuse, rejection—you know what I'm talking about. Jesus Christ Himself gave us stern warnings about hurting little ones. Abusing a child creates terrible memories that will haunt him or her into adulthood. Hurts of childhood, however, are not the only ones to generate devastating memories. Adults routinely hurt each other.

A woman I know was married to a man who continually neglected her. She suffered a chronic depression for sixteen years; then he finally decided to leave her. It took nearly six months of intensive work to get her past those years and years of sour memories, the repeated hurts he inflicted in a hundred ways. But her biggest hurt, we discovered, was being ignored as a child. She found it easy to excuse her parents; they were busy. But that did nothing to lessen the pain and emptiness.

Humiliation and Shame

Technically, these could be classified as hurts. Humiliation certainly is painful, and a lot of abuses produce humiliation. Every human being is vulnerable to the pain of intense humiliation, even thick-skinned toughies. Humiliation, especially in a sensitive area, is devastating! So I prefer to put it in a class by itself.

A college boy I know prided himself on his scholastics. Before the whole class a proctor falsely accused him of cheating. The class had 400 students in an auditorium-sized lecture hall, but the accusation would have hurt just as much in a class of three. The boy lapsed into a bitter depression for three years. He dropped out of school and pumped gas at a minimart. Finally, a friend of mine asked him, "How many years of depression do you think it will take for you to get even with the proctor?"

Horrors and Other Fears

Fear of abandonment. Fear of death. The specter of disease. And those are the normal ones. Children suffer a complete set of fears that are a natural part of growth and development. My colleague Paul Warren and I explain them in detail in *Things that Go Bump in the Night*. But horrors and fears can stretch well beyond those that you normally think of. Phobias take a heavy toll. Witnessing a violent act, a severe accident, a death, or maiming can generate bad memories that linger one's entire life. Apart from the horror of the incident itself exists the underlying terror, *That might be me next.*

The most important fears deal with people and relationships. Particularly in children, personal relationships are primary. Horrors and fears that eat into those relationships cause terrible memories.

More than one person has told me, "*Real* Christians don't fear. 'Perfect love casts out fear.' "

And of course, it's true, but how many of us exercise 100 percent perfect love?

Too, there are the fears God gave us to protect us from our own folly. By denying imperfection and God-given fears, such persons bury the fears deeper within, so that they become all the harder to root out. Too many of these people then also dump a heavy load of guilt on top of the mess: "If my love were perfect, I wouldn't have this fear." It just doesn't work that way.

God-given fear? Let me illustrate with some of my favorite animals—horses. Do you know how dangerous a horse is? Accidents happen. Horses behave like horses and get themselves and their riders into some big trouble. I have a healthy respect for horses, and I always handle them carefully. So do my daughters. But that doesn't mean I am free from fear. When I see my kids on horseback, I know the potential danger, and I fear for their safety. Fear is an automatic, God-given protective response. All life is dangerous, so God programmed common sense, caution, and fear into us. That cautionary fear, of course, is not the fear the Bible verse discusses.

Anger causes bad memories also. Anger is actually a form of fear, although the person furious because of someone's slight or misstep doesn't recognize it as such. Anger at its deepest level is a fear of being emotionally hurt. You strike out before you are struck.

God knows, literally, how horrors and fears can devastate us. Three hundred sixty-five verses of Scripture tell us specifically not to fear. Fear not. Fear not. "Fear not, for I am with you unto the end of the age." God is aware!

Hates

What a broad category this is. In addition to the feelings that might first come to mind when you think about *hate*, you also must remember that one of the most powerful of them is self-hate.

I recently saw a woman who, before she was twenty-five years old, had several abortions. Let's call her Karen. The hurt, the bad memories, and the guilt penetrated deep, deep down. She married and bore a child, a delightful little boy. One day a senile elderly man approached the boy in a manner that could have been construed in sexual terms. The man had no idea what he was doing, and the incident passed almost before it began. Certainly the whole thing ought to have bothered Karen somewhat, but she overreacted. She went ballistic, stepping over the line into psychosis. (Let me emphasize a point here. As I mentioned earlier in this chapter, anytime a reaction to an event is drastically out of proportion to what would be an appropriate response, either overreacting or underreacting, trouble lurks. It's something we look for, and you should too).

Obviously something sexual haunted her past. We started digging. At the bottom we found an intense hatred for herself. I had never seen hate quite so vivid. The self-hatred had her dwelling upon every wrong she had ever done to the point of self-destruction. Nothing can hamstring happiness and a person's effectiveness as a servant and worker quicker than bad memories.

How Bad Memories Erode Happiness

In the plaza of a city in Spain, bullfighters erected a statue to the British bacteriologist, Sir Alexander Fleming. It's not so strange when you think about it. Until the 1940s the greatest killer of matadors in the bullring was not being gored by the bulls *per se*—the *comada*—but the resulting deep infection.

Sir Alexander discovered penicillin.

People in developed nations have pretty much forgotten about infection. Major wound? Hit it with antibiotics. But in the absence of the miracle drugs, infection has dramatic and lethal effects. The bacteria that enter a wound at the time of injury multiply exponentially. They cast off toxins as wastes and by-products, poisoning the system. The body fights back valiantly with a variety of defensive weapons, and pus is literally the dead bodies of billions of cell soldiers, both bacterial cells and body cells. The person runs a fever because higher temperatures help the body in its fight. The infection spreads internally, far beyond the original injury, and can cause gangrene (literally, rotted flesh), septicemias, and death, even though the wound itself was not fatal. It's just the same with bad memories.

A man I once talked to defended the verbal abuse he dealt his children. "Life is the pits, and the sooner they find that out, the better. Nobody's going to pat you on the back in real life, but you better believe they'll be all over you if you mess something up. I'd be lying to the kids if I pretended it was any other way. Let 'em learn. Let 'em get used to it now."

He could not grasp how the ugly memories he planted in his kids would fester and poison their lives. By the age of four or five, children have a pretty good start on the shaping of who they are and what they want. We are beginning to see that this shaping begins prenatally. And yet, kids start out with no defenses at all to blunt abuse or ward off emotional damage.

When that man told his kids they were stupid or clumsy or bad, they listened as if his was the voice of God.

Worst of all, those messages undercut his children's only real defense in childhood against the slings and arrows of outrageous fortune, their self-esteem.

"I am sick of hearing about self-esteem, and low self-esteem and all that," fumed Elaine Houser in an unusual display of anger. "It's not scriptural. 'The heart is deceitful above all things and desperately wicked.'" She flushed slightly. "I forget exactly where that is."

"Jeremiah," I prompted her. "And how about, 'I am a worm and no man,' in Psalm 22. The Psalms are just about my favorite part of Scripture for casual reading. Is that the opinion God wants you to have of yourself?"

"Isn't it?"

I didn't get into the worm theology we discussed in my seminary days before medical school. Instead, I told her the story in Numbers 13, where Moses sent spies to check out the Promised Land before the children of Israel entered it. Ten of the spies said, "We were like grasshoppers in our own sight, and so we were in their sight." Talk about low self-esteem! Grasshoppers.

Only two of the twelve, Caleb and Joshua, disagreed. "We can do it! If God is pleased with us, He'll lead us in." You see? High self-esteem. Call it confidence. They were certain they could handle the enemy so long as God's help supported them.

You know the end of the story. Caleb and Joshua entered the Promised Land leading the new generation of Israel. Every other person from their generation died without seeing it. Think what a lack of self-esteem did to those thousands and, just as important, what it may be doing to you.

The messages in bad memories, especially the very early ones, can be sapping your potential before you can get anything going. The generation of timid doubters died in camp. Low self-esteem will destroy your chance to fulfill your dreams (the

Israelites yearned for the Promised Land in vain) and will derail God's dreams for you. He wanted His people to enter into the land of milk and honey even more than they did. Low self-esteem ruins relationships also, both yours and the Israelites'. The people wanted to stone Joshua and Caleb.

Obviously, your lack of self-esteem is going to sabotage your Christian service with a defeatist, "Oh, no I can't do that!" attitude. "I could never pull such a big project off." Well, it's true, you can't—not so long as you're thinking like that.

The infection that the verbally abusive man planted in his children might not show on the surface. As the body sometimes manages to wall off an infection, forming a cyst, so the mind walls off emotional hurts. But the infection remains, producing its toxins. The children have already been shaped by this father's ugly attitude toward life. They can escape it in adulthood only with great effort and pain and much struggle.

Will those kids simply forget with time? Perhaps somewhat, but the shaping will have been completed long before then. Might they build a wall of denial about their father's attitude, as sometimes happens? Possibly, but probably not. Denial occurs in drastic cases but not often in what you might call chronic situations. There is, however, one more way in which the mind deals with memories. That is to simply blank them out altogether. Seal them past recovery in a more thorough way than denial can achieve. In that kind of case, the memory appears to be altogether missing.

This was the situation with Ron Houser that worried Elaine. It could be harmless; it could mean a great deal. Let's examine Ron's case, and some others, in detail.

Why Some People Have No Memories

"It's a blank." Ron Houser was attempting to describe his memories of childhood. "I'm sure I went to school, but I can't remember any teachers and only one classmate, sort of. He's the kid I grew up with. And I remember him mostly from junior high on. Elaine thinks something's terribly wrong. I think the only terrible thing is my memory."

"It was a blank." A woman we'll call Hannah was describing her memories of childhood. "I had no idea what was festering inside. When I had my first baby, Christopher, I started getting these recurring nightmares. Anxieties. My midwife said it was just postpartum depression. 'Don't think anything about it,' she said. But I was asking myself, why would the birth of my son do all that?

"In my nightmares I began to see cultic objects. You know. Satanic stuff. I was terrified. And then a lot of horrible memories came pouring in like a flood." She still turns pale talking about it, and her son Christopher is four years old now.

"It's a blank." A fellow six feet three inches tall with tattoos on nearly every available surface of his body was describing his memories of his teen years. Let's call him Rhino. "I started smoking at eleven. Tobacco, two packs a day. Grass every day. Pretty soon I was into meth and acid. Coke when I could get it. This was before crack and the newer stuff. It was a blast! But I don't remember a ruddy minute of my life between the ages of fourteen and nineteen. I couldn't even remember it very well when it was happening. I'd have to call up a buddy the next day and ask him if I had a good time."

All three of these persons were aware of lengthy gaps in their memories. But why did these gaps occur?

Some people have wonderful memories and are able to recall details of the earliest past. Others, like Ron, can't remember eighth grade graduation. That's all normal. After all, there are sumo wrestlers, and there are people so puny they need help to put the cat out at night. Tremendous variation in physical build suggests that, similarly, tremendous variation in the raw ability to remember is to be expected, not marveled at.

The Lack May Be Normal

Ron turned out to be one of those people who simply cannot remember certain things. He needs a calculator because he never could memorize his multiplication tables. He can't remember phone numbers for thirty seconds. But he is very good at that part of memory that recalls skills and how to do things. Show him once how a transmission goes together and from then on he can fix any transmission in the world. He read an article in a magazine describing oscilloscopes and with no further help built one. He uses trigonometry with casual skill.

His past? It's a blank because his episodic memory simply does not connect. I assume the record is in there somewhere, but the triggers necessary for its recall are not.

It is also normal for early memories to be fragmentary. Paul Meier, for instance, recalls railroad tracks and running. He remembers being delighted because "Dad couldn't catch me." He also remembers that during an emergency of some sort, his dad walked back and forth, thinking about what to do. Bits and pieces. Disconnected vignettes. It's normal.

I can remember some of my grade school teachers but not others. Loss or absence of memory may be no real issue.

The Lack May Be Organic

Rhino, the bruiser with the tattoos, just plain fried his brain. He admits it. Drug-induced damage is permanent in that once the connections in the brain are destroyed they cannot be replaced. Sometimes the brain compensates by using undamaged areas to perform the functions the damaged parts once handled. That's an iffy situation; sometimes it works and sometimes it doesn't.

Accidents, trauma, and certain diseases can physically destroy part of the brain's storage area. Anything stored in that area, of course, is then gone as well.

Physical or hydraulic pressure on brain cells kills them. I've had the sad experience of watching people with inoperable brain tumors steadily decline as the tumors grew, pressing upon more and more cells. A head injury may cause, for instance, a subdural hematoma, a pocket of leaking fluid—blood and lymph and cerebrospinal fluid—that makes the membranes lining the skull bulge inward. The growing bubble of fluid presses on nearby brain cells.

Starving your brain cells will kill them also. Strokes do that. As you know, the blood carries nutrients and oxygen to your body's cells and takes away the cells' waste products. Some body cells can suffer an acute lack of oxygen for a while and do just fine despite a buildup of wastes. Brain cells cannot. They need oxygen constantly. A stroke occurs when one of the arteries feeding the brain becomes clogged, as with a blood clot or a glob of fat. Every cell from the clog on out suddenly receives no fresh nutrients, no oxygen, no waste disposal. Within six or seven minutes, those cells are dead forever, never to be replaced. If a large artery closes down, the person dies as a major part of the brain stops functioning. When small vessels plug up, ministrokes and minor strokes result. By and large, they affect only small areas of the brain. Rate of recovery from such strokes can be excellent if not too much critical brain matter is affected.

However, any information recorded in the affected area is lost along with the storage cells. That information has to be relearned. Episodic memories of the past cannot be recreated and, therefore, cannot be relearned. They're gone.

Once a memory is established, is it there forever? Only if its storage container remains intact.

The Lack May Be a Defense Mechanism

Here's the one to camp on. Ron can't do a whole lot about his inability to remember the past, and he really isn't interested in working on it anyway. After all he lived his whole life without knowing his third grade teacher's name. No big deal. Rhino isn't struggling with a defense mechanism. His problem is cell loss. But lack of memory caused by defense mechanisms in the brain require attention because not only are they possible indicators of repressed memories, they are adjustable. Fixable.

These defense mechanisms are built right into every person. Picture yourself getting your finger caught in a slamming car door. Pain! The fingernail in this case turns purple and green and black. Until the new nail grows in, a matter of many weeks, you have that black nail as a reminder of the accident. But not the pain. Although the finger may be swollen and tender for a while, it stops hurting fairly soon. Pain lasts only a brief time compared to the long time healing will require.

Not so with memories. Bad memories keep on hurting and hurting unless the brain somehow blocks them. Also, God doesn't want us to lie to ourselves, but there is simply too much to see if we perceived all of the truth all of the time. Call defense mechanisms a God-given cranial circuit-breaker.

The system sometimes goes awry, a typically human condition. The brain has some sinful defense mechanisms to protect us from the knowledge and pain of our own wrongdoings. To find peace with God we must get past those too.

And herein lies a problem. How can you tell if there are missing memories lurking undetected, damaging you, messing you up, if the defense mechanisms prevent you from detecting them?

Signs of Repressed Memories

When Hannah's son Christopher arrived, she began experiencing anxiety that she never felt before. Something new was happening in her life, something beyond what reason would dictate, and she got scared. The sudden anxiety brought her to us. Hannah experienced more than just nightmares and anxiety. She also showed evidence of several other items on our list of possible symptoms. Her husband, in fact, had a lot to say about her obsessive need to control.

We dug down into Hannah's past to recover a chilling series of episodes she had not suspected. When she was about eight, her older brother got her involved in a satanic cult. She had no idea about satanism at that time. It seemed neat because her older brother, whom she worshiped, said it was great. She was sworn to secrecy. The unspeakable acts she witnessed during the few years of her involvement culminated in the murder-sacrifice of an infant. Traumatized, she recalled none of this until her own son was born. When she looked at the newborn in her arms, those suppressed memories came crashing back to the surface.

As a rule of thumb, the more a child is traumatized or abused, the more of childhood that child will forget as he or she grows up. Isn't that a form of healing? When the memories are effectively removed, you no longer have to deal with them.

It doesn't work that way.

To quote David Seamands, "You want to disown crippling memories. In fact, you must. But you cannot disown them until you own them."

In psychological parlance, to own something is to accept that it exists in your life and acknowledge its influence. When you own your anger, for example, you admit that you are angry and that anger is a factor in how you handle a given situation. You own your sexuality by accepting that you are a sexual creature. You do not have to exercise your sexuality or your anger to prove you have them. Knowing you have them is sufficient. Only when you own your bad memories can you resolve them.

Time does not heal all wounds. Certainly memories subside with time, but they do not evaporate. Over and over in counseling we discover that everything that happens to you does something to you.

So let's tackle the bad memories and turn them into something positive. Left to fester, they will cause physical ailments, as we have seen. They will hamper your ability to function well. They will rob your happiness.

"Now just a minute, Doctor," I've had people remind me.

"Character problems are taken care of in childhood. 'He who spares the rod hates his son.' There are many such verses in the Bible."

And that's correct. Responsible parents can handle that sort of thing. The problem is that Gretchen didn't remember her parents as being responsible guides and counselors. That was her whole point.

Bad memories are one of the things that quench the Holy Spirit within us. Bad memories blind us to the Spirit's teaching and leading. In 1 Thessalonians 5:19–22, Paul warned believers to avoid quenching the Holy Spirit, but he also urged them to test everything and to hang on to what is good. We will do that very thing. Believe it or not, there is good to be derived from bad memories.

Not quite likely your brain is already adequately handling many bad memories. Just because you brain isn't doing it the way you think it should is no cause for alarm. Let me illustrate.

A friend of a friend was puzzled by the strange ways her grandson was developing. He was her first grandchild, an absolutely precious little boy. Doctors determined he was severely autistic. The woman was crushed. "It would have been easier for me had it been my son rather than my grandson," she confided, and she was right. But she went through an intense grieving process and got on with her life.

Then a major wildlife art show came to her town. As she attended, admiring and studying the fantastic pieces there, she was overwhelmed with the thought that her grandchild would never have a chance to do something like this. It floored her, and she had to go through the grieving process all over again.

Memories of a beloved deceased relative might be triggered by the strangest, most unexpected things. At first the tears come in torrents and then small glassfuls. That doesn't mean the bad memory of the death is causing problems. In fact, it's not. Grieving is necessary. So don't expect to dismiss forever every bad memory. Rather, understand what kinds are likely to cause trouble.

7

Preparing to Mend Memories

Sad, sorry Sisyphus.

Sisyphus in Greek mythology was condemned to roll a heavy boulder to the top of a hill. Struggle. Sweat. Strain. Just as he would almost reach the top, the boulder would break free and roll back to the bottom. Down he would go to begin again the arduous task of rolling it upward. Over and over and over.

"Oh, yes! That's how it feels. Over and over and over." Gay Strom nervously picked up her purse (for the fifth time) and plopped it in her lap. She is the Housers' neighbor I mentioned in chapter one, the widow who never forgot a grudge or slight, however small or ridiculous. "Just like Sisyphus. I think I have the problem licked, and the memories come rolling right back. Then I start feeling angry and upset all over again. And I can't just leave them behind. I'm trapped." She put her purse down on the floor beside her feet. Again.

She's not the only one.

David Seamands recalls his life as a missionary in India, "I saw men and women come to Christ. And yet the usual ways of building grace in new believers—meditation, prayer, Bible study—just didn't seem to work well in some cases." He discovered that the people who were having difficulty growing, who did not respond well to the usual methods of learning and developing, were being hindered by their past. Under the protection of prayer, he very carefully probed their memories with them and helped them uncover bitterness. As he brought those memories to light in a state of prayer, he showed the new Christians that God was present then as well as now. The revelations brought emotional healing as well as spiritual healing and growth.

If you were to undertake a major project, you would make some preparations first. You would obtain materials, dig out the right tools, set yourself up. We will do that kind of preparation before you try to heal your bad memories.

Prepare Thoroughly

"All right, but I've been through all the 'instant fix' advice. I've tried so many times, I don't feel like trying again. But I know I should. Are you sure I can get the boulder to the top of the hill this time?"

No, not sure. We hardly ever guarantee results, but we almost always get them.

The prospect of changing a bad past may seem hopeless to you. Your discouragement is justified; memories are very, very powerful. But nothing is impossible with the Lord. As the first step in preparing for the healing process then, you must ask yourself an important question.

Do You Want To?

"Of course I want to!" Gay protested. "I just said I wanted to, didn't I? Well, sort of."

It's not such a far-out question. A lot of people, deep down inside, prefer to loll in their misery because they are afraid of the pain they know will come as they pull free of it. It's like knowing it's time to take an adhesive bandage off a hairy spot. It's a scary thought! Besides, as miserable as misery is, it's familiar. It's handle-able. And what if others, perhaps loved ones, are hurt by the revelations that emerge? That's just as scary.

"I suppose that's scriptural." Gay, who attends a weekly Bible study with Elaine, is just as cautious and skeptical a scholar.

It certainly is. Jesus had to ask a man who had been ill for the last thirty-eight years if he wanted to be made well (John 5:6). The desire to be healed is not always a foregone conclusion, especially if the person has gone unhealed for a long time. The dysfunction now fits comfortably, in a twisted way.

Gay had serious health worries as well. Colitis, a condition characterized by extreme lower intestinal problems, plagued her, as did migraines. Also, her doctor was monitoring her erratic heart rhythms with an eye to intervening if the condition got any worse. These physical problems, Gay assured me, had nothing to do with her grudge-holding, and they were being attended to by other doctors. She was coming to me to ease the mental anguish.

I asked the question of Martha, a woman in her early thirties struggling with memories of early sexual abuse. *Do you really want to be healed?* Believe it or not she waffled on the answer. "I think I'm doing all right on my own," she finally said.

Counting on my fingers, I listed her recent episode of psychosis, her failed relationships, and the rocky nature of her marriage. She decided healing was better, but it took her awhile to come to that decision.

Once you decide to do something about it, the next decision is *what to do?* I suggest that you find someone to walk along beside you.

Find Someone You Trust

There are many ways you can approach the mending of memory, but the one way I never recommend is *alone.* You might venture to the brink of a severe pitfall without knowing it. An outside observer can often see it coming before you do. He or she can be there if the going gets really rough.

However, it should not be someone embroiled in the memories of your past. Until you have someone who can walk with you and yet be separate from the memories, you will find it almost impossible to lower your defenses and make yourself vulnerable. Ideally, a counselor trained in memory recovery is the partner to trust. He or she will know how to lead you gently through the process, will pick up on nuances and phrases that you may not notice, and can tell if the experience is going to be too much for you.

In the absence of a counselor, choose, preferably, a same-sex friend. If at any time during the process either you or your friend sees danger ahead, seek professional counsel immediately.

What is danger? If at any time for any reason you think about suicide, that's danger. Get into a hospital immediately. The hospital staff can handle it, and you're safe there. They can use medication, if needed, to pull you back from the edge.

The threat of a nervous collapse or psychotic episode is danger. Normally, the friend sees this coming before the person does. Call a halt and get help before going a step further.

An excellent alternative is to get in with a group.

Consider the Power of a Group

Gay nodded approvingly. " 'Where there is no counsel, the people fall; but in the multitude of counselors there is safety.' Proverbs something."

A group is many eyes and many minds to watch for pitfalls and hear unspoken messages. Groups are an excellent way to get past denial. They allow a nonpersonal sort of confrontation. "I'm not the only one who sees this; we all see it." The group can set you straight. It's one of the best ways to cut through excessive denial. The group will help you cut through transference issues too. A group member gets mad at someone who did nothing—that is, something triggered deep memories—and the group will pick up on it. Another individual might not, particularly if that individual is the person who received the anger.

A group can better recognize if something is about to surface that is perhaps beyond the experience of an amateur counselor. Remember, you need someone who can handle psychosis or even suicidal thoughts if they erupt.

Groups can allow identification. Just as you are thinking, *I am the only one*, someone else relates a similar experience. You're not alone after all. This encourages vicarious learning. You see how someone else succeeded or failed, and you thereby see ways you perhaps can do it.

A support group provides a safe and caring environment in which to explore the depths. It provides help, often something as simple as someone putting an arm around your shoulders to say, "I care that you're hurting." Support like that is a powerful, powerful thing.

How do you find a group? Ask at church. Do others want to explore memories also? Quite possibly they do. By forming your group out of fellow believers, you'll find the atmosphere will be enhanced by the similarity of faith that is built right in. A local clinic may be able to help you connect with one. Ask a hospital chaplain what's available. Sometimes the local librarian can help. I am often amazed by what a good reference librarian can find out.

Invoke the Holy Spirit's Help

Placing yourself under the cover of prayer is not just a precautionary measure. It is essential. Do it each time you set forth to explore memories.

You don't have enough faith in God to trust Him with this? Take this step anyway. Whether or not you believe in God or trust Him, He plays a major part in your life. Enlist Him.

If you are a Christian, I don't have to tell you God is good. You know that. He doesn't want you to get in over your head, and He desires all good things for you. Memories are so powerful you must lead them forth from the depths carefully, or they will crush you. As you do it with Christ's spiritual help, He will protect you from receiving too much too fast. You need His perfect guidance for what will be revealed, how you will deal with it, and how quickly the process will occur.

Fred Littauer, coauthor of *Get a Life Without the Strife*, recommends keeping a prayer journal. He advocates the use of written prayers—not for God's sake, of course, but for yours. Write down exactly what you are asking of God. Journaling is always a good idea, spiritual implications or no.

What do you ask? Tell God you are now ready and willing to go to work on bad memories. Ask Him to accompany you down the pathway to those memories, opening up what He wants to show you. Remind Him that you realize the two of you can face it together.

Gay took this step reluctantly. She knew much about the Bible but very little about trusting with her heart. Martha, the abuse victim, belonged to a denomination that does not place much confidence in the power of the Holy Spirit. She had no problem praying for guidance, but she had no real faith that anything would come of her prayer, either. Still she was ready to begin.

Search Your Memory

Bring forth as much as you comfortably can, the earlier the memories, the better.

Here is where a friend is invaluable. You know the principle of brainstorming, where three or four people get together and toss ideas around until a plan or project takes shape. Your partner can prod your memory—*not* put things into it—by asking questions to draw things out.

Once Martha got going, she was easy to draw out. Most people love talking about themselves and about early memories.

"What about first grade?" I asked. "Remember anything from first grade?"

"Oh, my, yes. There was this playmate, Johnny Warden. He broke his arm and came to school with it in a sling. He got *so* much attention and status from that broken arm with the kids gathered around him asking questions and the teacher making over him. I remember my envy. I wanted so much for my arm to be broken, so I would get some of that attention."

A few more questions like that got the river running. And then it suddenly stopped. "Fourth grade," I urged. "You'd be about ten."

"Nothing, doctor, not a thing. Everything is so clear until then."

"Describe your fourth grade room."

"I can't. The others were so vivid, and that one's a blank. Not fifth grade, either, and I know it was a new school because we moved. I should be able to see it."

"What was going on at home then?"

Do you see what I was doing? To draw out memories without drawing too violently, I asked about surroundings, home, school, the places the child of a particular age would feel familiar in. I asked general questions about what she remembered and also specific questions, such as asking her to describe her home life. What were siblings like? Pets? A favorite toy or pastime? Who lived next door? Where was a favorite place to play? Give your friend biographical facts to ask details about and memories may come. One bit of recall usually leads to another.

The blank spot at ages ten and eleven was significant because Martha's memories before and after that time were numerous and clear. During these years her mother, a widow for the preceding four years, briefly married. The marriage was over in two years—the two years of Martha's dearth of memories.

After we skated around the edges awhile, I led her back to those blank years. Again, I started with the biographical facts—the name of her school, siblings, favorite things and places. As soon as she said, "I can't remember," I would ask something else, jogging her recollections.

In one memorable session, she vaguely remembered a dark shed. We talked about the sensations in that shed—the stale smells, the cool, powdery dirt floor, the little shafts of light streaming in through cracks between the vertical siding boards. Actually, she did not specifically remember those sensations. Her adult mind told her they ought to be there, but she could not honestly come up with childhood memories.

Now, a dark spot in otherwise retrievable memories is a warning flag. Here is something the memory has deliberately blocked off. I'm talking about denial. Why deny access to a shed?

Eventually we ascertained that in the shed an elderly neighbor had deliberately exposed himself to her. "Did he do more than just display himself?" I asked.

"Yes."

And the torrents came, floods of tears and floods of memories. He lived across the alley behind them, and he would wait for her. Should she venture outside for any reason, and her mom seemed constantly to be sending her out there—to throw away the garbage, or get clothes off the line, or bring in her younger siblings' toys—he would be waiting. He showed her a gun one day and threatened to shoot her mother if she ever told anyone. Now, many years later, she still half feared he would appear out of nowhere and shoot her mom because she had just betrayed the secret.

Was it silly to still fear that old man? Not at all. She was bringing back a ten year old's memories, not an adult's. Her memories of that time had never surfaced until now and thus had never been reworked the way most memories are. Our memories don't just lie there, you recall. They mature as we do. In that child's mind, the old man's danger loomed very large.

I also worked through this step with Gretchen, the woman who grew up working, working, working. She had no such problem recalling her past. Her persistent memories of constant drudgery, of always seeing another job she had to do looming on her immediate horizon, infuriated her. "My father wasn't interested in building character. He wanted a slave. He was the king, and he needed a subject. And Mom didn't say a word or lift a finger to disagree with him. Why should she? I was doing her work as well as my own. I did all the laundry and changed the beds from the age of nine on." Her voice became higher and harsher. "I *hate them both!*"

Because Gretchen seemed to have no blank spots or especially touchy spots in her past, I led her in a different way than Martha. We explored memories she had of her parents' lives. We looked at biographical information and tidbits of family lore that she did not experience firsthand. Her mom suffered diphtheria at the age of eleven, she recalled, and they nearly lost her. Her dad was a wild young man, partying and crashing sports cars, until the Depression hit and straightened him up. Survival has a marvelously sobering effect.

And finally there was Gay, whose problem was just the opposite of Gretchen's and Martha's. Gay remembered too much. The pain of snubs and wrongs stabbed anew, as if all had happened yesterday. We spent quite a bit of time not dredging up the forgotten past but cataloging all the memories she wanted to unload.

All three of these women were ready for the next step.

Identify the Other People

Write down the names of people who are part of your memories. Whom exactly do you remember? Gretchen and Martha did so. Gretchen listed her mom and dad, and her two brothers who were both considerably older than she and in college by the time she was ten or twelve.

Martha listed neighbors and a third grace teacher.

Gay took a certain delicious pleasure in writing down the people who had done her wrong. For years she had been battling these memories. Suddenly she was reversing herself and encouraging them. It didn't take her but a second to get turned around and into the swing of it.

As you explore your memories, jot down significant and not-so-significant people. You may not remember their names. If not, try to identify them in some other way, such as, "the lady across the street with the gray wig" or "the guy who used to stand out in his front yard for an hour with the hose, watering his grass" or "the kid with the funny hair who stood around in front of our house and picked his nose."

Identify the Problem

We are going to apply what are essentially methods for conflict resolution. That is: identify the problem; identify you reaction to it and your part in it; and determine what you will do or refrain from doing to resolve it. Remember that when you are resolving a conflict, you cannot make the other party change (unless that other party is three years old and the conflict involves a clearly defined no-no). Similarly, you cannot make the memory be something it is not. We are going to deal with the memory as it is, as you remember it.

First you must describe, in a single sentence if possible, what you think the problem is.

"I'm a workaholic," Gretchen said.

"I was sexually abused," Martha said.

"I have physical ailments," Gay said.

Good start! While you're at it, identify the filters through which you view the situation.

Filters?

Think for a moment about how a photographer uses a filter. Filters in photography are colored or treated glass that fit completely over the lens to change the image. For example, a polarizing filter cuts out all the light entering the lens at a certain angle, making the scene sharper and the colors deeper. A photographer will use a polarizing filter on, for instance, a mountain scene in which haze would otherwise make the distant mountain appear dim. A yellow filter makes a colored photo yellowish but brings strong contrast to a black and white shot.

Memories fall short of being videotapes of the past in a very important regard; they have been filtered through the perceptions of the person "taping" them. These filters change the whole picture, not just portions. Age is one of these filters.

Age Changes Perspectives

Let's pretend you remember falling off a horse when you were six. Its name was Ginger. The memory of that event has matured as you grew up by being reprocessed through the maturing perspective. It has faded as the years shoved it farther and farther away. But most important to remember, it was originally recorded by a six year old. The event was seen, literally, through the eyes, feelings, and perceptions of a child.

When you remembered the incident as a seven year old, you were still a little scared of that pony, but it didn't loom quite so large. After all, you had grown several inches. By the age of ten, you viewed the whole memory with a more mature perspective. And now, here you are an adult, vowing never to put your own child on such an unruly little beast as Ginger.

Certainly, maturity changed some elements of the memory. That's what maturity does. It switches filters, so that although the facts of the memory are not changed (you did indeed fall off), the feelings and perceptions which accompanied the fall change. In adulthood you realize it wasn't a horse. It was a Shetland pony that seemed as big as a horse to that small child. You now recall that the pony was the stubbornest thing in three counties and given to bucking. You couldn't have chosen a worse mount for a six year old. But you didn't think that at the time as you do now. And that's what maturation is—a growth of understanding. Maturation by itself, however, usually will not completely alter the memory of an event.

Memories also are recorded from only one point of view— the recorder's. All other perspectives are not recorded in the memory.

Memories Differ According to Point of View

This particular filter made all the difference in the world to Gretchen, the woman who had to work from childhood on. In fact, it was the key to her healing. It is the key for many people.

Gretchen brought her brother Reinhard along for one session. "Hardy," she called him. She and Hardy talked about their parents.

"I'd call Mom the laziest woman in the world," Gretchen said.

"Oh, I wouldn't," Hardy said. He shared Gretchen's round face and clear, pale skin. His eyebrows and hairline resembled hers so much that if you considered photos of them from the eyes up, hair length aside, you would be hard pressed to tell the two apart. "Mom was permanently weakened by the diphtheria she had when she was a kid. The poor woman couldn't clean and jerk a pencil. I remember once watching her get an iron frying pan out of that drawer in the bottom of the stove. She had to brace her elbows on her knees and grip the handle with both hands. Even so, she almost couldn't haul it out of there. I took it out of her hands and put it on the stove for her. I was seven."

"How do you know how old you were?" I asked.

"I remember I had just come home with one of those apples my second grade teacher always gave to kids who won the daily spelling contest. I had to put the apple down to pick up the pan. Yep. Second grade."

Gretchen was staring at Hardy. They had never discussed memories together before. "You're saying she was feeble?"

"Yeah. Not mentally," Hardy said, "just her muscle strength. I was stronger than she was almost from when I started school. Don't you remember Pop ranking on us? 'You kids will never give your mama a single moment of trouble or you will hear from me. Do you understand?' You better believe we understood."

"You mean that's why she always said, 'Wait til your father gets home'?" Gretchen asked.

"Sure. We kids could have tied her to the railroad tracks anytime we wanted to. She couldn't spank effectively. That's why she had those sinkers on her flyswatter."

"That flyswatter!" Gretchen said. "I was so embarrassed by that! I'd think, 'We're such a weird family we can't even have a normal flyswatter.'"

"Wait!" I interrupted. "Sinkers? Fishing sinkers?"

"Yeah." Hardy's eyes shone with pride. "Pop was a genius! Mom had good aim—she could swat a fly dead on—but then it'd stand up, sneer at her as it brushed itself off, and fly away. Half the time she couldn't put enough muscle behind the whack to hurt it. So Pop pinched regular old lead fishing sinkers onto the flyswatter handle, up near the blade, so that the inertia of that extra weight would give Mom's blow more oomph. He was really clever at things like that. He would think a problem through and come up with an unusual solution."

Obviously, Gretchen and Hardy were raised by two different sets of parents. Hardy's heroic mother struggled valiantly against debilitating weakness. Gretchen's was lazy. Hardy's father cleverly and admirably triumphed over the nasty little vicissitudes of life. Gretchen's ruined her childhood by constantly cracking the whip. Why did such radically different memories come from two siblings?

You'll recall that Gretchen's father led a wildly profligate life until the Depression. We learned from Hardy that the man nearly starved when the stock market crashed. His pampered existence became a hand-to-mouth struggle, and the experience jolted him drastically.

He told Werner and Hardy more than once that he deeply regretted wasting his youth and intelligence, and he urged the boys to avoid his error. "Get an education, develop some skills. Be ready if for any reason you are suddenly cast upon your own resources. Contribute to the world, don't be a taker." Why did he not tell Gretchen this? He did. But she was too young to grasp what he was saying.

Hardy and Werner were born a year apart, and Gretchen was born six years later. In many ways she was an only child. When Gretchen entered junior high school both her brothers were in college already. Also, enough of the Old World culture lingered in her parents that they treated sons somewhat differently than a daughter. The sons were encouraged to greater independence at an earlier age.

You see then why Hardy's memories of his parents differed so greatly from Gretchen's. He bore no animosities because he had few of the experiences she recalled so vividly, and he harbored proud, fond memories she never experienced.

Using What You Know

The stage is set, the preparations complete. Using what you now know and the resources you've identified, you can at last dig into your memories and work seriously at healing the bad ones. Consider yourself a person cleaning the attic or the garage. You riffle through boxes, picking out the "good stuff" and discarding or mending the useless things. We are ready to commence the healing process.

Healing bad memories. Isn't that lying to yourself? They are there. They happened.

Lying? No, never. You don't want to lie to yourself. Indeed, God does not want you to either. Healing memories does not mean changing them so that what did not happen becomes remembered as something that did happen or vice versa. Healing memories mostly means making peace with the past. It can be achieved in any of several ways. Let's look at them.

8

Healing Unhappy Memories

Memories are valid. And memories lie.

Your brain records every single thing. And your memory fills in major blank spots.

Your memory is your best friend; without it you could not function. And your memory keeps you from functioning.

I love paradoxes!

When two things are true, and yet they are opposites or mutually exclusive—that intrigues me. And memory is so wonderfully complex that it lends itself to all kinds of paradoxes.

One of the deepest paradoxes is that bad memories can yield good fruit.

Martha, the young mother who as a child was sexually molested by a neighbor, absolutely orbited when I suggested that. "You can't mean that! Do you realize all the years I suffered with the shame and guilt? And hatred. I hate that man. I hate my mother for letting it go on. I hate her even though it's not really her fault. She didn't have a clue. My life would have been so very different if that hadn't happened."

She's quite right. It messed up her life and robbed her of joy. I didn't say bad memories are the best thing that can happen to you. We would no doubt be better off without them, at least without the truly wrenching ones. But that does not mean they are worthless. In the process of healing your bad memories, let us also use them to your benefit.

As you begin, be cautious of anyone who is pushing heavily for memories to come out. You can go overboard, forcing things that should not be surfacing so rapidly. You need to keep a healthy balance lest you be overwhelmed. There is another reason to exercise caution, and that is to not allow suggestions to alter what your mind is bringing forth. A lawyer in court would call them "leading questions," designed to plant thoughts in the mind of a witness. You want your memories to be your own work alone.

A good place to start the actual healing process, once the preparations have been made, is to get a new perspective on memory. Gretchen already did that in her conversations with her brother Hardy. It was a blessing that Gretchen's brother attended our session that day. His appearance provided the jumping-off place for her first step in healing her memories. He showed her a different perspective. Perhaps you know someone who can perform that service for you.

Seeing the Situation from All Sides

Picture yourself, your siblings, and your parents standing about at random in a large room. No one's view is exactly the same. Most of you have your backs to at least one or two others. The only way to know what everyone looks like is to describe each other.

"Mom, your hair looks nice with that new do. Wavy and natural. I never noticed until I saw you from the back."

"Dad, from the side you look like Lionel Barrymore."

"Chris, there's a big black bug on your back."

"Aaaa!"

Obviously, Chris's describer is a sibling.

Do the same thing now, not with people but with memories. Look at situations and people from some perspective other than your own.

Someone Else's Point of View

This altering of perspective was a real eye-opener for Gretchen. "I never realized any of that which Hardy was talking about," Gretchen confided. "This changes the whole way I see my parents. Now I understand why I was the one who washed the car and mowed the lawn and all. Pop was too busy making a living and putting the boys through school, and Mom physically couldn't. She looked normal. I never guessed about the weakness. Just this revelation has done a lot to ease my bitterness."

Note that this first step does not pertain to everyone. It did not apply to Martha, for example. Martha could look at her ugly memories from the viewpoint of the man who did her such harm, but his crime remained a crime nonetheless. Her parents' indifference and failure to heed her unspoken cry for help remained the same memory it had always been. The technique that was so much help to Gretchen would be of almost no help to Martha.

As Gretchen saw her parents' struggles in the new light, she could forgive them quickly and easily. At last she understood. Although the abuse existed, it was done innocently, out of caring on the father's part, out of necessity on the mother's part. Not so Martha. Even if Martha could stand before her tormenter and hear his explanations of why he did what he did (nearly every abuser has some rationale for his or her behavior), it would not change her perception. No amount of rationalization can erase the damage done by sexual interference.

How about you? Others are not perfect. Neither are you. We live in a fallen world. We are, therefore, all fallen. Jesus Christ lifts us up spiritually, but we can lift each other up in other ways. Your parents were not perfect. That is exactly the point to remember.

Think about your childhood from your parents' point of view. (Incidentally, when I say "parents" I may actually mean, in your particular case, "surrogate parents." You may have been raised by persons other than your biological or adoptive parents. If that is the case, keep in mind we're talking here about the people who actually raised you.) In other words, pretend you are your parents trying to raise a kid who was you. To get you started, ask these questions:

- What obstacles did they encounter, financially and in other ways, during the years they were rearing you?
- What traits in you did they fail to understand?
- Which ones did they understand only too well?
- What did your parents do wrong?
- What did they do right?
- What sacrifices did they make?
- What dreams went unfulfilled?
- Would you say the wrongs were deliberate, or were they born of ignorance?
- Did carelessness or preoccupation play a part?

Let these questions jog you into asking more questions. Spend some time playing with this switch in point of view.

Now consider your parents' shaping influences.

What were *their* parents like?

- Attentive or neglectful?
- Distant or close?
- Generous with time or too busy?
- Given to hugs and laughter or dour?
- Strict or permissive?
- What traumatic events did they endure?

- Other factors?

How did that influence the way you were raised?

- Were your parents like their parents?
- Did they copy the parenting methods their parents used?
- Did they bend the opposite way from the way they were raised (for instance, being very permissive because they considered their own parents overly strict)?
- Was their parents' influence excessively strong upon them even after they were out and on their own?

Did your parents abrogate some or all of their parenting to their parents, your grandparents? (i.e. Did your grandparents play a major part in raising you?)

- They did, to a large degree.
- They did not. The grandparents had little or no contact with me.
- I believe my grandparents played a healthy, moderate role in my upbringing.

These questions and similar ones can help you understand your parents' motivations and actions. They may never have discussed things with you. They may have told you one thing, perhaps to "spare" you, when a wholly different reality pertained. Understanding these realities is healing for many people.

Now that you are in the swing of it, expand this examination beyond parents and grandparents. Many people besides your immediate family shaped your life. Explore the roles which friends, family members, and neighbors played in your memories. How were their attitudes shaped? What traumatic events struck them? Did the ripple effect from those blows affect you? How much?

The more you pursue this sort of exercise, the better you can understand the driving forces and motivations of others in your past. What do the events of your memories look like from their point of view? Perhaps, like Gretchen, you will benefit immensely from becoming aware of the reasons other people in your life did what they did.

"That still doesn't help me," Martha said. She had achieved a good balance in her emotional life and was working hard to heal her memories. "What about those of us whose bad memories stem from people who acted wickedly, maliciously?"

There is another point of view you must consider carefully. Your own.

Your Own Point of View

Martha said, "I think my point of view is clear enough."

"Bear with me on this," I urged her.

First, let's examine the role you believe you played in the family. You are probably aware that children adopt certain roles to a greater or lesser degree, although the purposes of the roles function below conscious level. The roles take form by age three or so, and the child has no conscious idea why he or she is doing certain things typical to a certain role. The important point here is that these roles also create a filter through which the child views life. Let me review them. Were you:

- The Perfect Child? Usually the oldest, the Perfect Child is the kid who can do no wrong. The pseudo-mature child. The straight A child. This child gives form to the family's pride and honor.

- The Acting Out Child? Often a second-born or middle child, this little imp is the vent by which all the family's pain escapes. This kid tends toward destructive and self-destructive acts.

- The Clown or Show-Off? Sure to get a laugh, this child is often the baby of the family. This terminal case of the cutes is designed subconsciously to divert the family's attention away from pain and sorrow.

- The Lost Child? If so, you were the one about whom everyone said, "Such a quiet, well-behaved one! I wish my kid were like that!" You blended into the wallpaper, never giving a moment's trouble. In effect, you had simply withdrawn from role playing, which is a role in itself.

- An Only Child? If so, you had to wear all the hats sooner or later, depending upon the occasion. You were more independent than most kids and more self-sufficient. You probably related to grown-ups better than did most kids and may even have had some problems relating to your peer group.

Determine where you seem to fit in your family's scheme of things. All these role-players are extremely good at reading a situation and playing it according to the role expectations. Kids sometimes shift places as they grow up or swap roles or adopt more than one in order to fit into new situations.

The role(s) that you adopted indelibly stained the way you perceived events around you. Even more so, your role(s) determined how you would react to the situations and events recorded in your memory. Although a child is helpless in the face of malicious, indifferent, or misguided acts of adults and therefore cannot change the situation, the role determines how the child feels about the event—the emotional response.

Every child tends to take on the guilt of the world, but the Perfect Child much more so. Because of the honor-bearing and the pseudo-maturity, the Perfect Child forgets a cardinal fact of life: Children have absolutely no power. No clout. The Perfect Child persists in thinking, down at the nethermost level, that somehow any tragedy could have been avoided had he or she simply done something differently. Anything can come out right if you only handle it right.

Gretchen was a Perfect Child, at least to a certain degree.

She wished a hundred different times that she could have changed the way her childhood went. "If you just handle it right. . . ." Gretchen felt at fault because she obeyed. And yet to do otherwise would have rubbed too much against the grain of a Perfect Child.

The Acting Out Child can tough it out. But behind that defiant exterior lurks one scared kid. The child doesn't really relish the acting out role. The Acting Out Child convinces himself or herself that this injustice, this evil, this terrible memory, doesn't really hurt at all.

The Clown absolutely adores the tragic opera *Pagliacci*. Right there is the Clown's life: "Put on your costume and makeup, get out there and wow the audience, and don't let them see the tragic interior behind the vestments." The outside is laughing and the inside is weeping uncontrollably, but only the Clown knows that.

The Lost Child never asserts, hardly ever reaches out. Whatever happened, the child sees no hope in easing the pain or sharing it. *Dismiss the trauma if you can and get on with life*, the Lost Child thinks.

Martha was a Lost Child. Over and over in her early days, she would hear adults tell her, "Well, you should have said something." Martha described to me a shopping trip to buy school clothes for her and her sisters. Her mom, frazzled, bought this and bought that and tried to keep a rein on both budget and her clamoring daughters' requests. But Martha didn't clamor. When they got home, everyone was outfitted except Martha. The money had been spent, and not an item of the new attire was hers. Her mom snapped in an accusing tone of voice, "Why didn't you speak up?" The message? Martha's silence, her reticence as the Lost Child, was at fault—certainly not Mom.

In her deepest being Martha was fully convinced that the man's molestation was her fault because she let it happen.

The Only Child's self-sufficiency is simply not adequate to

carry burdens of pain that even adults would find onerous. And yet that self-sufficiency is what the Only Child depends upon. Gretchen in many ways was an only child because her brothers were so far detached from her in age, gender, and interests. Gretchen's conscious self thought that it could handle her festering anger and resentment. Her subconscious, in a cry for help, deliberately got her a shoplifting conviction. Depend upon it: Your subconscious will get the attention you need one way or another.

Because bad memories were filtered through the childhood role, they can be turned around by viewing them from the perspective of another role. After all, if you had grown up in a different role, the memory wouldn't be quite the same because the filter of that memory would be different. And should you change your role, you will no longer react the way you used to.

"Change?" Martha shook her head. "I've been the way I am my whole life. No way I'm suddenly going to become a clown or something."

"True," I said. "As Dr. Kevin Leman and Randy Carlson say in their book *Unlocking the Secrets of Your Childhood Memories*, you can't change the grain of the wood. That's set. But you can change the shape of the piece carved from it. Awareness is a powerful thing. If you can become aware of how your role altered your perception of bad memories, you can alter them again with new perceptions."

Martha frowned. "I see. It's like the person who benefits from seeing an event from someone else's point of view. Except that both perceptions are *my* point of view, old and newer, not others'."

Exactly.

This will require some deep digging on your part. You have to find out what your original perceptions were and in what ways you can change them. Because such things as false guilt and shame are buried so deep, they are hard to find. Here's a clue for getting started.

A woman I know does all the hiring interviews for a major firm in Fort Worth, Texas. She said, "When I ask a job aspirant one of my key questions, I usually sneak it in under the guise of small talk or peripheral talk. And one of those key questions concerns the aspirant's opinion of other people. I ask casually about the people this aspirant worked with and under in the previous job. If the person is fresh out of school, I ask about classmates and teachers.

"If the aspirant praises his or her bosses and coworkers, that says pretty nice things about the aspirant. But if the interviewee ranks on and on about what turkeys those people are, and how awful the boss was, and 'they're such jerks,' da da da, that tells me very little about the others and a whole lot about the aspirant. People tend to view others the way they view themselves."

Conversely, you view yourself the way you view others. Examine how you view others, then, as a clue to how you view yourself. Are you an eagle, finding it difficult to fly with turkeys? Or just the opposite?

The way you view yourself now is very likely the way you saw yourself in early childhood. This matter is worth some deep thought. What were your perceptions of others? Think about that. How do you think they perceived you? Keep in mind that the memories are filtered through the very attitudes you're trying to uncover. Essentially you're trying to see the filter itself.

Analyze what is imperfect about that viewpoint. Those imperfections colored and distorted your early memories. Finally, take some time—quite some time in fact—to consider what your memories would be like had they been framed ("taped," if you like) through the filter of a different attitude.

As an exercise, you may wish to choose a specific bitter memory of your past.

- If you are any type other than a Clown, think about how a Clown would perceive your memory. How would a Clown handle the feelings that memory evokes, such as sadness or guilt?

- If you are any type other than an Acting Out Child, how do you think you would see the event? What would an Acting Out Child have done and felt?

This exercise leads us to our next point.

Play Act Other Endings for the Scenario

"That's trying to change the memory, isn't it?" Martha asked.

"No," I said. "It helps you understand that, as a child, you had almost no real options. It helps you get past that deep, deep feeling that 'If only I had done such-and-so, it wouldn't have happened.' And also, it softens the memory as you dream about what might have been."

The new endings, the imagined ones, need not be happily-ever-after endings. They could be worst-case scenarios. Those things happen too, and quite likely the actual ending was one of the better possibilities. That in itself is comforting.

In a sense we are reremembering the memory from a wiser, more world-aware, more rational adult perspective. Keep in mind that children are not rational. Until age six or so, a child doesn't fully differentiate between fact and fantasy. What that child imagines is just as real as actual events. Early memories necessarily reflect that irrational childhood perspective. We are recasting them to a more realistic perspective.

While you are doing this, give yourself a pep talk. Tell yourself that all these if only's and ought to's are conjecture. Even if they seem legitimate, they are fantasy. Had they been put into practice they might have saved the day. *Just as likely, they could have precipitated tragedy.*

You cannot second-guess a child's memory long after the fact. You no longer know enough about the situation. If only Martha had cried out, for instance, the man might have withdrawn and not bothered her again. Far more likely, he would await another chance, perhaps do her even worse harm, perhaps concoct a story to make her the villain. Her mom and others might have believed him, an adult, over her, the fanciful child. That's what usually happens. "If only" and "ought to" *must* be removed as permissible alternatives of thought.

An observer might claim that Martha could have screamed and kicked and run the first time the man approached her in a lascivious manner. No, she could not. She was physically capable of doing that, yes. But children are slaves to their nature. Emotionally she was the Lost Child, the child who did not kick and scream and act out. She was the quiet one, the good one. She hesitated because of her very nature. And her abuser seized that hesitation to make his threats. The threats of violence precluded any further resistance on her part.

Analyze your motivations for what happened. Let's say that you suffered an ugly incident because you were paralyzed with fear, or something happened because you were afraid and failed to act reasonably or heroically. *For a child the fearful response is a right one.* Fears are programmed into children for a very important reason: It helps them survive. Children are not to be called upon to protect themselves; that is the parents' job. The children's job is only to recognize the danger. So if fear is a major ingredient in an early memory, that's good. It's supposed to be.

I was able to show Martha that her suffering came from a highly admirable base. The threats of harm were not against her but against her mother. She was submitting to violation in order to protect her mother. That is the highest sort of altruism and most commendable, especially in a child.

Do you remember that Paul wrote in 1 Corinthians 13:11, "When I became a man, I put away childish things"? He was speaking of spiritual insights primarily, but emotional insight is just as valid. What we are trying to do here is put away the immature, negative, destructive way the child in us remembers ugly events.

I was helping Martha get past the crippling effect of thinking she could have prevented the abuse heaped upon her or reversed it somehow. Those thoughts were as much a part of her original memory as were the events themselves, and they were one of the most destructive elements of it.

Here comes the hardest part. After this, it's all downhill with your feet off the pedals.

Forgive

It is important to forgive everyone who had a hand in forming your bad memories.

"You've got to be kidding!" Gretchen gaped.

"You've got to be kidding!" Gay snarled.

"You've got to be kidding!" Martha shouted. "That old man? I can't! Do you realize what he did to me for two years? Not a shred of remorse, either. The only reason it quit was because Mom left my stepdad, and we moved. No. Huh-uh."

Forgiveness is an integral part of any effort toward a better memory.

This is a book concerning memories, not a book on forgiveness, so I will go only briefly into details of the forgiveness process. Those details are available in several excellent works offering help in a variety of formats. One example is the book *Free to Forgive*, providing you with three hundred sixty-five devotionals to help with both behavioral and psychological steps. If you are working with a counselor, the counselor can guide you through the process.

The purposes of forgiveness are threefold. They are to free you from the grip of the past, to restore your relationship with God, and to let you move comfortably into the future. Forgiveness is absolutely essential, and it rides almost exclusively on memories. An incident, attitude, or situation happens and then is gone. The memory remains. It is the memory of the incident that is to be forgiven.

Forgiveness is much easier taken in increments. The first increment is to **acknowledge the hurt**. This was incredibly easy for Gay Strom; in fact, it was her problem.

Next, **commit yourself to genuinely forgiving the hurt.** And this step, for Gay, was incredibly difficult. That also was her problem.

Deliberately speak the words (or write them), "I forgive you, [Person], for [the occasion]." Say the words several times if necessary.

Then, **commit yourself to the conviction that you will not seek redress or retribution.** "If I could gain redress, I would," Martha vowed. "But I can't, so the issue doesn't matter." Actually, for Martha it did indeed matter. It was her attitude I was asking her to change, not the actual prospect of redress. She had to deliberately turn herself away from the desire to seek it.

Gay also claimed, "It doesn't apply to me. There isn't any means of doing it or even any appropriate retribution to take." Perhaps so. Still, Gay had to take this conscious and deliberate step.

The next step is contingent upon whether it would be appropriate: **Confess the hurt and confront the person responsible for it.** Sometimes it would do no good, as when it would hurt more people than it helped, for instance. Sometimes it's impossible, as when Gay's husband died, or Martha lost contact with the neighbor. To complete this part of forgiveness, weigh the results of the various kinds of action you might take: writing a letter, calling, confronting face to face. What will happen? Who else will be hurt?

If you choose to confront, do so with extreme care for the other person as well as for yourself. If you choose not to confront, write a letter and tear it up or burn it. You have confronted the person in the letter. You've gotten it off your chest, so to speak, but you've done no further damage to others.

"I hate writing letters," Gay mumbled. "I even send cassette tapes to the kids instead of writing."

So she spoke her confrontations not in a letter but on a cassette tape.

At one of our sessions she grinned—for the first time in years, she claimed. "Do you know how weird a cassette tape looks as it shrivels up and burns?"

Finally, **put it behind you.**

This does *not* mean forget! For one thing you cannot forget, so it's no use trying. For another, forgiving it is an important growth step for you and does not deserve to be forgotten.

One last increment is the crowning achievement: **Open yourself up to relationship.** Your relationship with the person was damaged, perhaps beyond repair. The Christlike action is to forego retaliation and animosity and mend the fences.

For Gay this wasn't too hard once she completed the process of forgiveness. She continually talked about how light and free she felt as she completed this step.

Let's pretend for a moment, though, that Martha still had access to the man who wronged her. Should she open herself to a civil relationship with him? Civil perhaps. Barely. But remember that his actions were criminal as well as unethical and immoral. Martha, and anyone else in a similar situation, would certainly protect herself from further criminal contact. She would in no way condone his actions. Forgive, yes. Allow, no!

The single greatest detriment to uncovering and mending bad memories is to fail to take the great leap of forgiveness. People become bitter. Martha certainly did. So did Gay. Gay in particular suffered serious physical problems because of her bitterness. Forgiveness is not erasing memories. It is choosing to not let them eat you.

Martha, Gretchen, and Gay all had to consider three groups of people they might need to forgive. So should you.

Parents

"Yeah, that's me." Gretchen found her parents easier to forgive once she realized the struggles they went through. She came to see that her life couldn't really have been any other way under the circumstances. But what if she had not found that revelation? She still would have to make forgiveness of her parents, even in her former state when she felt so bitter, the next crucial step.

Spouse

What role has your spouse played in all this?

"Not a thing," Gay grumbled. "Right up until the day he died, all he did was ride me about my constant griping. As if he didn't gripe. You should have heard him. Even on his deathbed."

Gay needed to forgive her husband. Forgive him for what? He contributed to her bad memories. All spouses do. It's not by design. It is simply that spouses are so close that they hurt each other on occasion. Can't be helped. A lack of sensitivity to the suffering spouse's feelings, or even an oversensitivity that irritates, deserves forgiveness.

Any other involved persons

Friends, neighbors, or relatives, particularly close ones, all need your forgiveness.

What part have they played in your life?

"Here's where I gotta do it, right?" Martha asked.

Here's where she had to do it.

Martha had no idea whether the old man was living or dead. She didn't know his name. She had no way of returning there to look for him. So she wrote him a letter.

She described what he did to her and how she hurt. Then she spelled out her forgiveness. She forgave the violation he perpetrated, the pain he was causing, the sorrow. Her tears flowed freely.

She shook her head. "I don't feel any better than I used to. It still hurts. In fact, I feel worse. He doesn't deserve forgiveness!"

"Will your letter ever be delivered?" I asked.

"Probably not."

"Will your forgiveness ease that man's mind?"

"Hardly. He doesn't know it's happening."

"Then for whose benefit is the forgiveness intended?"

"Mine, obviously," she said. "But shouldn't I feel better about all this?"

Forgiveness is never dependent upon feelings. It is an active step the forgiver takes, whether the one forgiven responds appropriately or even knows about it. Gay took it. Finally, Martha took it too. With that step she released her memories from their dependence upon the past. She discharged a responsibility God requires of every human being. "Forgive us our wrongs / shortcomings as we forgive those who do wrong against us."

One other person she would have to forgive was God Himself.

"Now that *is* ridiculous!" Martha fumed.

Not at all. She would forgive God for one of the same reasons she forgave the old man—her own well-being.

God need not be forgiven for anything because He never errs. How often do you have to forgive someone for something he or she did even though it was not a mistake as such or was done without malicious intent? You forgive anyway. God presents a more extreme case, but the principle is similar. Forgive Him not for His imagined imperfections but because of your (and this is true of all of us) imperfection in seeing His purposes and will. It is for our sake we forgive God, not His. And He honors that.

Along with forgiveness I recommend prayer for help in understanding His will and why He failed to intervene in a situation that caused you pain.

Let us assume you consider yourself a child victim. And because children are so utterly dependent upon the adults in their lives in every regard, you were therefore not responsible for the abusive situation. You still need to take the next step.

Accept Your Responsibility and Forgive Yourself

"Wait!" Martha cried. "You just said I was not responsible. You've been drumming it into me over and over."

The victim's responsibility in any situation consists of that victim's response to the victimization. Sounds circuitous at best and confusing at worst? First, consider that your response to a situation from your past is a powerful shaping influence in your life. How you respond the next time depends upon what you learned specifically from the abusive situation last time. Your brain uses your past responses as models for more recent responses. When your ball bounces, in other words, it will bounce in the same direction each time. Most, usually all, of this happens below conscious level. Along with specific learned responses, your brain learns general responses as well— to hate, to resent, to fear, to escape.

Now think how many years and how much energy you have wasted on fear and misery and hatred. Unproductive emotions. Unproductive actions. That is why you ought to forgive yourself, not the situations of the past but the inadequate and useless responses you've been making because of them. By forgiving yourself you lay these past responses to rest. You can move forward with a clear heart.

"But it was so unjust to do that to a little girl. To let that happen to a little girl," Martha said. "So much injustice."

"Let Jesus be your ultimate example," I said. "He instituted communion so that His people could be part of Him just a few hours before the ultimate act of injustice. Healing is built into that. Accept the healing and go on."

Dispel Bad Memories

"Dispel." Gay didn't look too certain. "What? You mean stuff them?"

No, no, no. You never just disregard bad memories and pretend they don't exist. They do. But put them in their proper place. With the act of forgiving you have pulled their teeth, so to speak. They no longer have control over you unless you let them. Don't let them.

An immediate way Gay might avoid dwelling upon her grudges and feelings of being slighted would be to simply think about some other memory as soon as one of the angry ones raises its head.

"It can be something very simple," I suggested, "such as walking in your front door and having your dog greet you. Something with pleasant connotations. Picture yourself going out your front door into sunlight, then coming back in."

"I could even cut a couple of roses from the bushes by the porch," Gay said.

"Exactly. I've seen memory called 'the ability to smell roses in winter.' Deliberately associate pleasant memories, whatever they are," I said. Most people can do well with just a little bit of encouragement in the right direction. Gay certainly did.

If your mind persists in bad memories of a person after you have forgiven him, that does not mean that your forgiveness failed to "take," or that you are somehow deficient. It means simply that the bad memories are too deep to oust easily. Sometimes facing the person responsible for the bad memory heals it. Let me emphasize that if you come face to face with a person you have a problem with, then for your sake as well as the other person's, confront him or her in a loving way.

Talking to a trusted friend or counselor can defuse the persistent memories. Like Martha, write a letter and burn it. Or perhaps write a letter and send it, but be cautious.

Beyond Healing

What are some of the fruits we promised which would follow the healing process?

Gay Strom saw some of the sweetest fruit. A year after she began working out those ugly memories of snubs and wrongs, her heart rhythm had stabilized and her colitis was, except for occasional rare spates, a thing of the past. Her migraines are very rare now. Gay is not an unusual case. Healing the memories heals the body.

Gretchen explained another aspect of healing well: "With my anger and resentment cancelled out, a lot of good memories surfaced that I had more or less forgotten about. Praise and pride. My father praised a lot. He was quick to reward a job well done. So did Mom, but because I resented what I thought was her laziness so much, I never noticed. She was always telling me what a good job I did or how nicely I did this or that.

"For the first time in probably thirty years, I remember how she'd read to me. I'd sit beside her in her big overstuffed chair, and she'd read and read for hours on end."

Gretchen was starting to develop a trove of warm memories as rich as her brother's. Those positive recollections had been there all along, but they were muted by the ugly ones. Buried. Martha, too, as she dealt with the bad memories and put them behind could find bright ones.

This is one of the best rewards of dealing with bad memories. Because they weigh so much, they distort not just the aspects of the past that they reflect directly, but all of it. When they are treated and healed, they take on a more reasonable proportion. Sure, you remember them, but now you can reflect on pleasant things as well. You are switching filters. And it's about time!

A second benefit extends beyond memories. As you work through all that garbage (and that's what much of it is) you grow in strength. Anytime you undertake a strenuous job and succeed, you grow stronger, and it's no less true here. Along with that general growth of character comes an improved relationship with God. Practicing forgiveness always does that because God is the author of forgiveness.

Healing memories makes us all function better. The person who is proactive instead of reactive can do more and do it better. That person seizes the day. When you heal old memories, you no longer react blindly to the past.

Only after Gay had learned to put those old grudges on hold and work past them did she learn how badly she had been reacting to them. "They ruled my whole life," she said. "I would avoid attending the social events because certain people were there. I refused to talk to some people. It was horrible!"

There certainly is a use for old memories. Dredged from the past for purposes of analysis, these memories provide the fodder for an assessment of the past as a basis for changing the future. The hurt may be there, but it's not there to dwell upon. To move past.

A cautionary note: Many people say, "After my first or second session of counseling I felt worse." Or, "When I started getting into this stuff, I thought I'd made a drastic mistake. It really hurt for a while."

This response is common. If a broken bone heals crooked or fails to heal at all, doctors have to rebreak it and reset it to straighten it. Believe me it hurts worse the second time! "I feel worse," you say? That's great! That means you're working on the issues.

There will be relapses too. I recall a specific instance when a patient, a middle-aged man, came to me in tears. He was doing well mending his memories of the Vietnam war. Then his wife quite innocently served him a Cajun dish, blackened redfish. The smell brought back the vivid memory of burning bodies in a disabled military tank. That particular food dish smelled almost that way to him. He still hates the dish. But there's not a thing wrong with the dish or with him.

Another young woman in a support group found herself facing flashbacks a year after she thought she had taken care of the problems that had produced them in the first place. She had, as it turned out. Now she was two years older, just entering full womanhood, and they were back because her adult self had not dealt with them.

She decided to try a relinquishment letter. She poured her heart out into a long, rambling letter. She wrote the feelings as well as the story. It ended with, "Lord, I know that what I cannot control I have to let go. I can't do anything about it. I have to give it to You." Then she took a match and burned it. This was to symbolize her release of the negative memories. Once she arrived at that point, she no longer found herself dwelling on those memories and others.

Depression enters into the equation as well. Everything seems to be rolling along okay, and then something goes wrong. The person gets depressed, and other bad memories flood back. When you feel depressed weakness results and that's when bad memories surface.

It's certainly nothing new. Elijah fled for his life to a hiding place in the wilderness with Jezebel's minions hard on his heels. He was certain he was the only person in the whole country who still remembered his Lord. He had to rest a while, eat, and then tackle life once more.

As people slide back, they feel as though every pit is the same. We see it all the time in counseling. But the pits are not the same. The lows are not as low, the duration not as long.

Building up a bank of new, good memories is the best way in the world to remind yourself that positive things are happening. The distance you have come does not show up clearly when sadness, weariness, and depression strike. Good memories provide perspective.

It is fair to look at negative and abusive memories like a physical injury. However you got it—playing football, falling down stairs, getting stepped on by a large horse—the scars and other remains of the injury are there for a lifetime. You better believe Satan is just waiting to bring up negative situations and feelings to use against you. A bad memory is always going to be there; but it doesn't have to continue to cripple. We learn to cope.

There is one class of bad memories I've not fully explored yet because they are not always regarded as such. Also, they behave somewhat differently. These are the obsessions, the memories that keep cycling round and round inside you. They deserve study.

When Memories Will Not Heal

Barry couldn't shake the image. He was thirteen, and his little brother Roy was three. They were playing tag in the front yard one Sunday afternoon. Barry would chase Roy and the little boy would squeal with delight as he ran away. Barry feinted and grabbed. The toddler lurched along with the endearing splack-splack-splack run of tiny kids who have not quite mastered running.

To escape Barry, Roy turned suddenly and ran into the street—into the path of a moving car. Roy died ten hours later. The memory of that one moment tormented Barry for the next eight years. At the age of twenty-one, Barry still had not completed his second year of college. He couldn't hold down a job. He repeatedly got into minor scrapes with the law, mostly traffic violations.

When he came to us, he said, "I know I can do better than this. I know I'm probably smarter and more responsible. But I can't help myself. Please help me!"

To paraphrase the wonderful words of the old hymn "Precious Memories," "Obsessive memories, how they plague us."

Not many people are plagued by obsessive memories, but those who are become trapped. They are not hopelessly trapped, but they are trapped. It is beyond their immediate ability to break free and move on with life. There are several reasons memories won't heal, and they deal largely with medical conditions.

Here is a sad twist on the revelation that memories can cause health problems; health problems can cause problems with memory.

There May Be Medical Reasons Memories Won't Heal

Medical reasons are not the only reasons people's minds are captured by persistent memories, but when the problem appears, they must be considered as the probable reason. One of the most common medical conditions we find is called an obsessive compulsive disorder.

Obsessive Compulsive Disorder

Harold drove his coworkers nuts. He turned "neatness counts" into a dogma. All his papers and books had to be lined up just so. His desk had to be absolutely perfectly arranged. If the pastor set the chalice down on the altar off center during communion, Harold went wild. And heaven help anyone who might accidentally spill coffee anywhere near him.

Harold's obsession with orderliness includes a memory element; he possesses an impeccable memory for everything he ever did wrong. Everything. Every detail. His wife left him because he had a near photographic memory for any mistake she ever made as well. "Life is too short for this guff," she told him as she walked out.

Meredith, a teenage assault victim, couldn't get the memory of that horrible moment to go away. The memory of the assault, still vivid many months later, played over and over in her mind.

A girl we'll call Angie was deeply depressed about her past.

She dwelt upon her failure to finish college. She dwelt upon her failure to marry one boy and her mistake in marrying a different man. She thought of opportunities lost, holidays ruined, and errors her parents made. No matter how hard she tried, she couldn't get past her past.

All these people were obsessed with memories in different ways, but they all shared common ground: although their problems were presented as psychological disturbances, a part of the cause was physiological—a chemical imbalance. Until their body chemistry imbalance was addressed and corrected, nothing they could do would ever get them past their problem. In each case the body was acting independently of conscious will.

However, Barry's compulsive memory did not share this common ground because his problem did not have a medical component. Some do, some don't. It takes a trained eye—a psychiatrist or other professional—to spot the problem.

But is all this something new, a creation of modern medicine? Over three hundred years ago, John Bunyan, as revealed in his autobiographical materials and letters, was an obsessive compulsive, totally hung up on certain details of behavior and theology. But it didn't divert him from greatness. He wrote *Pilgrim's Progress*, one of the world's great pieces of literature, still in print in three hundred languages.

Finding the Cure

Obviously, if obsessive memories hammer away at your happiness, the first step in overcoming them is to obtain professional assurance that a medical cause is not part of the problem.

In Meredith's situation her memory circuits were constantly cycling. Her problem was psychological and also spiritual. She doubted God's existence for quite a while because He permitted the assault to happen, but she was already suffering a serotonin imbalance. That is, a hormone present in both the brain and the blood (it's involved in clotting) was not doing what it normally does. The medical condition can arise for any number of reasons, and she didn't realize it was happening. The assault tipped her over the edge. Fortunately, serotonin imbalance can be corrected with medication. A counselor was able to help Meredith heal her memories once her body allowed the healing to begin.

Serotonin imbalance also contributed to Harold's obsessiveness. In fact, he had twice tried counseling at his wife's behest, to keep her from leaving. But it didn't "take." The reason it didn't take was because the constant cycling was chemical. We first broke the cycle and then the healing began.

Angie's depression, we found, was due in part to a low level of norepinephrine, a hormone that affects neurotransmitters. The memory connections kept connecting essentially at random and there was nothing she could do about it. Adjusting her hormone balance ended the random connections.

But what if you have no chemical imbalance, no miracle medical correction that can give you a jump-start toward recovery? You want desperately to get on with your life and stop replaying the past. How do you contain and control those impeccable memories about wrongs done to you and things you did wrong? The person harboring such memories can become literally obsessed. Fortunately, there are several practical things you can do.

Ask God's forgiveness for your mistake

No matter what situation you are in, take this step first. What you think about God does not change who He is. He can get along just fine without you. But you desperately need the assurance that He has forgiven you.

Can you have that assurance? Absolutely! One of God's most magnificent promises is that if you truly seek forgiveness, it is yours. Forgiveness is not dependent upon a feeling or mood.

Either you are or you aren't forgiven, regardless of how you happen to feel, and God assures you that you are if you ask it of Him.

"Well, gosh, I don't feel particularly forgiven," then, is not at issue.

How do you receive forgiveness from God? Ask.

"Lord, I beg You to forgive [this event] that has been weighing so heavily in my life. I am sorry it occurred. Thank You for forgiving me as You promised You would."

Because I personally am committed to Jesus Christ and walk with Him, I know without a doubt that He forgives my wrong-doings. But there are days when I just can't feel that He's near. That's my shortcoming as a human being, not His doing. He is never distant from me; no matter how I feel, God will do His part. You can depend on it.

The second step you should take is to find someone trust-worthy with whom to talk about it.

Talk it out instead of burying it

"What a lousy idea!" said Barry, the man who saw his little brother hit by a car. "The more I talk about it, the more that hideous memory will stick. I'm trying to get rid of it, not intensify it!"

I then asked, "Is it losing power?"

"No," Barry said, "it is not."

Talking about it brings it to the surface. Again, in psycho-logical terms, to own a memory is to accept its existence and admit its power over your life. Discussing it and talking about it with someone else is one of the best ways to own something. Barry could not alter his incapacitating memories until he dragged them up to the surface where they were accessible. For years he tried to stuff them down deep, and it simply did not work. The further they were driven down, the more they festered. Their negative influence was impeded. Barry had to bring them out where he could see them.

But what could he talk about with a friend, mentor, or counselor? (By the way, God Himself is the perfect friend, mentor, and counselor.)

He could describe the memory itself.

He could discuss the aftermath of the incident, the time immediately following the tragedy, and what advice he received from others. He could ask himself and his counselor whether, in retrospect, that advice seemed good and sound or bad and damaging.

He might talk about how his memories have haunted him.

He could—and should—discuss how he could change his life and get on with it if the memories were put in their proper place.

"Why?" Barry asked. "There's nothing I can do about it. Roy's gone. It's done."

There sometimes are things you can indeed do about a bad memory. Sometimes restitution is possible.

Provide restitution when it's appropriate

Barry could not bring Roy back, but he could seek other ways to make restitution, if not for others' sake, then for his own. For example, he had never acknowledged the part of the neighbor who saw the accident, called emergency services, and ran out to administer first aid until the EMTs arrived. She still lived in the house two doors up from his folks' place. He could send her flowers and a simple card to thank her for helping.

When is restitution not appropriate? When it would hurt or hinder someone else. Barry's sister, then fourteen, also witnessed the accident. She stood on the porch with her hands pressed to her face and screamed. She kept screaming for nearly fifteen minutes until a paramedic dragged her into the house. Afterward she was immensely shamed by her actions. She wanted to think she would act sensibly or even heroically in a situation like that. Instead she behaved like, in her words, "a real head case." To send a card, flowers, or other remembrance would be cruel.

Finally, Barry could deliberately pull the plug on the hold those memories exercised by limiting time spent on them.

Set a limit on time spent with the memories

"Oh, sure," Barry said. "That's the craziest suggestion yet. I just say, 'half an hour today and that's it,' right? Get real."

It's not quite like that, but Barry had the general idea. This step depends upon a good execution of steps one and two. You have to enjoy the assurance that the negative actions in the memories are forgiven, and you have to own them. Bring them to the surface. Once they are on the surface, in conscious thought, they are manageable.

For some people it helps to simply set aside specified time to work on it. Then those people refuse to deal with the memories at all other times. Perhaps you might tell yourself you are going to let the memories intrude on Saturday, but not on any other days of the week. When they pop up on Sunday or Tuesday or whenever, you send your mind off into other thoughts immediately. It takes some practice. But you can do it if you completed steps one and two.

It usually does not work to merely banish obsessive memories. They don't banish. That's burying them. By giving them a limited place in your life, then holding them to that limit, you break their obsessive nature.

Reluctantly, Barry committed verbally to giving his obsessive memories three hours on Sunday afternoons. He had already spent considerable time with a respected uncle talking about the events that plagued him. His uncle was wise enough to offer no platitudes and no advice. He simply listened well. Barry's memories had surfaced; they were owned. This step would not have worked otherwise.

Again I remind you that this approach will not work if there is a physiological factor in a problem involving obsession. These steps would not have worked at all for Harold or Angie. Only medicine could break their destructive cycles.

Barry was employed part-time as a guard at a minimum security facility. He went off duty at 3:00 P.M. Sundays. Obeying his commitment he sat down with the prison chaplain at 3:10 the next Sunday, and they talked about the obsessive nature of his memories. At 6:10 he took the chaplain out to dinner, and they talked about other things. The next Sunday he and his uncle went bowling. The memories were one of the topics of conversation. The other six days of the week, as the memories appeared on the surface of his mind, he literally dismissed them until their proper time.

To Barry's amazement, his memories accepted the limitation. It wasn't easy at first, but over a period of a month or two they had lost their grip. Today, Barry is within a semester of finishing a bachelor's degree in criminology. He met a young woman, a rookie officer employed as a jail matron at the same facility where he works. She knows all about his obsessive memories; she's one of the persons with whom he discusses them.

But only on Sunday afternoons.

Avoid Getting Stuck

Barry was already stuck in his memories, which is essentially what obsession means. Because bad memories happen to us all, and never at convenient times, it is important to avoid getting stuck in them to start with.

Barry was in his early teens when the accident occurred, so he would not have been able to go through avoidance procedures on his own. He was too young, too untried. At that age he would need a trusted counselor to lead him down the road. An adult, however, can probably handle it.

I urge anyone in this situation to pay attention to feelings.

If you feel that this is not working or that the situation is more than you can handle or you're afraid to move through this, seek help! Many times people come to us as a last resort. They would never wait until all else fails before they took a toothache to the dentist or a broken leg to the hospital. Not all suffering is physical.

If Barry had received counsel at the time of the accident or soon thereafter, the first thing we would have worked on would have been guilt.

Identify and Manage Guilt

The younger a child is, the more strongly false guilt grips. Kids are absolutely certain that they are the reason for anything wrong in the world. At thirteen, Barry would not yet have left that attitude behind. We would therefore begin with that particular kink in his thinking. Barry was riven with guilt.

Among Christians, especially older Christians with a solid theology, we find an extra dimension to guilt. Many feel guilty about not forgiving themselves. The theological theory is that Christ already paid for any wrongdoing. It's not theory, of course; it's fact. But accepting that fact is difficult. So many Christians give lip service to this important truth while down inside they keep hitting themselves on the head, punishing themselves even though God already took care of it.

As it turns out, Barry truly accepted God's forgiveness and release from guilt fairly easily.

To ease the acceptance of forgiveness I often refer to Psalm 51. David was a man after God's own heart, but that did not save him from committing a great sin with Bathsheba. David was far from perfect. He said, "For I acknowledge my transgressions, and my sin is always before me" (Ps. 51:3).

See? There he is in the stuck position. But then he goes on asking God to cleanse him and to hide his face from sins—to create a clean heart. Then he accepts the gift *he already has* and goes on to praise his living Lord. By accepting the gift of forgiveness and cleansing from guilt (that's what cleansing is), he can get past his stuck position. So can you.

Deal with the Bad Memories Promptly

After establishing the guilt resolution or at least getting it started, we can work on the memory itself, using the basic steps found elsewhere in this book. Because remote memories, memories from the distant past, are more global in storage and not stored near short-term memories, they are harder to deal with. Barry had ten years of memory accretion to take care of. Had he been able to deal with his memories at the time of the accident, he would have had much less rooting out to do later in life.

The best part of mending the past is building that new trove of good memories to fill the boxes in your attic.

With what shall we replace bad memories?

"Why replace them?" Barry asked.

"To supplant them, which means you'll want new memories substituted for bad. Good memories," I said.

We already established that bad memories that are not dealt with will poison relationships—damage children's memories and transfer to the mate; there are all sorts of nasty ramifications, and they will cause bitterness. There is no magic, though, no verse to memorize that will make all bitterness go away. One of the most important steps to getting rid of the bitterness is reprogramming your brain with new and positive things. You have to fill the vacuum left behind by mended and banished memories.

To explain that comprehensively, and not just in Barry's case, let us turn from exploring bad memories to building and regenerating good ones. It is important, if possible, to start right at the beginning with early childhood.

How in the world can you do that? Let's explore options in part three, "When Children Remember."

WHEN CHILDREN REMEMBER

10

Shaping Young Kids' Memories

Astrange beeping sound fit comfortably into the equally strange dream Ron Houser was having. Then Elaine was poking him violently in the ribs.

"Ron! That's the smoke alarm!" She was scrambling up out of bed.

Still groggy, Ron sat up. Fire!

Their seven year old, Stephanie, was calling from the kids' bedroom, "Mommy? I can't make Chad get up!"

Elaine yelled, "Stay there! I'm coming." She was patting down the closed door feeling for warmth. Ron watched her drop to her hands and knees, open the door and crawl out into the hall. Chest-high smoke came drifting in.

This is it. This is the real thing. Ron stood there, numb, trying to think what to do first. Elaine was already after the kids. There were those contracts and building permits on his desk. He couldn't afford to lose them. Or the backup diskettes with all the quotations and cost breakdowns. Wait. Those figures were all on the laptop too. All he had to do was grab the laptop.

A window shattered in the kids' room.

He ran out into the hall and immediately took a deep breath of smoke. *For crying out loud, Ron, wake up! You know the rules! You've drilled the kids often enough!* He dropped down and crawled three feet toward the office before he turned around. Too much smoke. He'd have to ask the firemen to get it.

Firemen! He turned and crawled rapidly back to the bedroom. He grabbed the cordless phone off the bedstead and crawled to the kids' room with the phone dangling by its antenna in his mouth.

The kids were not here. Elaine wasn't here. He climbed through the open window and ran out to the street.

Shaking, Stephanie and Chad stood on the curb by the mailbox, greenish in the sallow streetlight.

"Where's Mommy, Steph?"

"Over at Gay's calling the fire department. Daddy . . . ?" The fear in her dark eyes made his heart ache.

He ought to hug them or something, but first he'd call the fire department also. Maybe Elaine couldn't arouse Gay. Gay was a prime grump and might not bother to answer the door if she was in one of her snits. Old Gay was half deaf anyway. Why did Elaine go there? That was stupid. She should go somewhere where they'd hear her pounding on the door. He punched in 911. The phone beeped steadily, its red indicator light blinking. He had to pause to think what that meant. It meant the battery was low. The line failed to open. He jabbed the hang-up button, jabbed it again, and stabbed in 911. Again it failed to connect. Furious and frustrated, he flung the phone aside. He heard it rattle the hydrangea bush twenty feet away.

Elaine came running across the street. He noticed she was barefooted, and she didn't have a bathrobe on. He wished she had paused long enough to grab a bathrobe, so that people wouldn't see her running around in a nightgown.

She stopped beside him, scooped Chad up, and pulled

Stephanie in close against her. The kids clung to her like Velcro.

The fire trucks came from the substation over on Melrose Street. You could hear the sirens when they left the station, whee-whooing and howling. Their air horns honked. *Firemen do love to make noise*, Ron thought.

The living room window shattered and black smoke poured out into the black night. If the fire were really big in there, Ron reasoned, you would see flames. He didn't. It was totally dark inside the house.

With a million flashing red and yellow lights, two fire trucks and a red pickup came around the corner off Thirty-seventh. Still holding Chad, Elaine took Stephanie with her as she crossed the street to Gay's front yard. The trucks roared up to the curb. Instantly, half a dozen fire fighters were laying line, calling to each other, running toward the house with masks on their faces and bulky air tanks on their backs.

The man in the pickup came jogging over to Ron. "Anyone inside there?"

"No. My wife, two kids, and I—we're all out," Ron said. He pointed to Elaine across the street. "Hey, see if your men can get my laptop out of the office, will you? That corner window right there. It has my whole business in it. I can't afford to lose that."

"I'm afraid we aren't going to be able to save much." The man wagged his head. "Your house is already fully involved. See the smoke coming out from under the eaves at the far end there? These older frame houses, once the fire gets into the attic, it runs end to end in minutes. Just praise the Lord your family is safe."

My family is safe. But my business is lost. So is my grandmother's china cupboard. And the two-hundred-year-old dry sink. And the organ. We paid a fortune for that organ.

Elaine treasures our wedding pictures and the photos of the kids growing up, and now they're gone. He glanced over at Elaine. She was wearing a winter coat. The kids were wearing coats of some sort. A neighbor woman was hugging Elaine closely with both arms. Every window on the block was lighted now, and people stood in quiet clumps all up and down the street, watching Ron's life burn up.

His was not the only perspective. There was Stephanie's. It had begun five minutes ago as his had.

Stephanie sat up in bed. What was that beeping? She heard it before, but where? The smoke alarm! Daddy was having another fire drill. He was beeping the smoke alarm to get everybody up.

"Chad? Get up! Fire drill." She hopped out of bed and got down on her hands and knees. "Chad!" She galloped pony-style over to Chad's bed and grabbed a handful of pajamas and shook. "Come on! We're supposed to get up."

Now she was supposed to feel the door to see if it was hot. She crawled over and put her hands all over it the way Mommy showed her. Cool, naturally, just like always.

But then she smelled smoke. Either Mommy was making this a special ring-ding fire drill or there really was a fire! "Chad, get up! Mommy? I can't make Chad get up!"

From far away, Mommy called, "Stay there!" Her voice sounded scared. Stephanie crawled rapidly over to Chad's bed and pounded on her little brother. Chad wailed and started pounding back.

When Mommy came crawling in the door, thick smoke poured in with her. She closed the door, stood up, and ran to the window. It stuck like always. Daddy said the wooden frame was warped. Stephanie could never get it open.

"Hide your face, Steph. I'm going to break the glass."

Stephanie grabbed Chad and hid him too. The window crashed. Stephanie just had to look! With lots of little clinks Mommy broke out the sharp, jagged pieces that were left.

"Come here, kids!" Mommy said. "Steph, you go out first and help Chad so he doesn't hurt himself." Mommy lowered Stephanie out into the chill air. Stephanie stretched her arms up. The streetlight gave enough light that she could see Chad's bare feet. Chad dropped, and Stephanie grabbed him. They ran for the mailbox, the outside meeting place, just the way Daddy taught them.

Out at the mailbox, Stephanie turned. "Daddy's not out!"

"Don't go back," Mommy said. "Don't move an inch, do you understand? I'm going to call the fire department." Mommy ran off across the street. A light was on in Gay's bathroom. Mommy pounded on the bathroom window. She shouted and nodded vigorously. The light from the bathroom window made her face yellow. Now she was running around to Gay's back door.

And then it was very lonely. Very, very quiet. Dark. *Scary.* Stephanie mustn't start crying or Chad would start crying. She was getting really cold too. After hours and hours, it seemed, Daddy dropped down out of Stephanie's window and came running. He had the cordless with him. He must not have remembered the battery needed replacing.

"Where's Mommy, Steph?"

"Over at Gay's calling the fire department. Daddy . . . ?" She so much wanted him to pick her up as if she were a little kid again, but he didn't. She wanted him to tell her it was all right, but he didn't. He tried to use the phone. The fury in his face frightened her.

She didn't get truly scared though until he threw the phone into the hydrangea bush. Things were infinitely worse than she thought! She had never seen him this upset and angry before. She was afraid of the fire, but most of all she was afraid of Daddy.

Finally, here came Mommy. She picked up Chad because Chad is smaller, but she let Stephanie hug against her, and that was almost as good. A couple times before she said Stephanie was too heavy to carry anymore. Stephanie regretted that now. She clung to Mommy.

Stephanie heard fire trucks lots of times as they went to other people's houses because they stayed over on Melrose Street, just a couple blocks away. Now they were coming to her house. Stephanie could follow with her ears, and when they came around the corner off Thirty-seventh, she could follow with her eyes. Who couldn't with all those flashing lights?

Mommy led Stephanie over to the curb in Gay's front yard. They could watch everything from here as the firemen dragged hoses and cranked open the fire hydrant on the corner.

It was all so interesting. Stephanie wasn't afraid anymore. Well, not very much, anyway. She remembered again how cold she felt; she'd forgotten it for a while. Mommy held her close and tight. Then Mommy put Chad down as Gay gave them all coats to wear. Peg, the neighbor on the other side, hugged Mommy the way Mommy hugged Stephanie, and Mommy began to cry. Stephanie wasn't certain why, but she began to cry too. Maybe because Chad was crying.

All the neighbors were out here now, watching. No wonder. It was exciting, and nobody was going to sleep after those sirens came through with all the lights flashing and men yelling. This was really kind of fun, actually. It was the most exciting and interesting and terrifying and weird experience Stephanie had ever had, and she would never forget it as long as she lived.

Kids' Viewpoints

Stephanie and Chad carry totally different memories of that night than do their parents, not because they were less obser-vant (in fact, kids are often more observant than adults) but because their viewpoints differ. Early childhood memories are shaped by early childhood itself.

Chad, at almost five, harbored some fears adults never think of. For the longest time he feared that the fire was all his fault, perhaps because he had been bad that day somehow. There was no rational basis for this. There didn't have to be. As I've said before, young children have global guilt. They are still so egocentric in their thinking that they assume they are responsible for everything that happens in their immediate world. Chad was also afraid that someone would take Daddy and Mommy away because they didn't have a home anymore.

Of course, that sounds silly to us. It sounded silly to Chad two years later. But at the time, that fear was very real to him.

Should you plumb the memories of Ron and Stephanie, Dad and daughter, two years after the fire, you would hardly recognize that both people were describing the same event. Ron, of course, saw the monetary loss and the loss of all the records for his home-based contracting business. These were staggering losses, many of them not insured, some of them irreplaceable. He saw the loss of valued, cherished things. Ron perceived the safety implications and how close the family came to the tragedy of death. Over and over he thanked God for that smoke detector.

Stephanie remembered darkness, fear, and the heady excitement of all those fire trucks and firefighters. She remembered her father's fury. She remembered her Mommy's strong hugs and the feeling of Gay draping the warm coat over her. She remembered the sight of her mother's face illuminated by Gay's lighted bathroom window. It was a week after the fire before she grasped that her favorite Barbie doll was gone forever, and that they would not be able to live in their home anymore. Structurally unsound, it had to be torn down.

Now, two years later, Stephanie was getting bad dreams about that night.

"I can't understand it," Ron said. "She handled the whole thing just fine at the time. We figured she was over it. Now all of a sudden, she's waking up in the middle of the night screaming. She's acting just plain nasty toward Chad and sullen. That's not like her."

That might not be like Stephanie, but she was reacting naturally and appropriately. Stephanie, older now, understood better the terrible danger her family had survived. She harbored a deep inner fear that the fire might come back, that her parents this time might be hurt. In other words, they were an older person's fears, fears she did not have the capacity to understand two years ago. Although they were delayed, emerging years after the fact, Stephanie had to work through them, processing them just as she did the original feelings and fears of that scary night.

To better understand this, let's look in detail at the difference between Stephanie's original perception of the fire that destroyed their home and an adult's.

Kids' Perceptions Are Based on Adults' Reactions

Let's pretend for the moment that what burned was not their home but an unused shed out back containing nothing of value. She and her daddy watched the shed go up, watched the firefighters do their thing, and shared in the excitement. Her father did not get visibly upset. He and Mommy philosophically kissed off the minor loss. He and Mommy, noticing that the children were frightened and uncertain, reassured them both verbally and physically. Stephanie would remember the fire as an exciting experience but not a terrifying one.

Stephanie's perception of that fire would have been vastly different, not because it was the shed instead of her home but because her parents were not distraught. As it was, she cried because her Mommy cried. More than anything else her father's unprecedented display of fury and frustration colored Stephanie's memories of the house fire. Children's deepest responses are not to situations but to valued adults' reactions to those situations. It is the children's primary learning experience and usually sets the stage for how the children will react in adulthood.

Kids' Perceptions Are Based on Feelings

Note the details of Stephanie's memories as described before. She remembered most vividly her father's emotional reaction. She remembered her Mommy crying. She remembered the warm, snuggly feeling as the neighbor put a coat on her. She remembered the excitement and all the other emotional responses. She did not notice that the heat blew the living room window out or that the house was seeping smoke end to end. It was the emotional attachments in her life—immediate family and, to a lesser extent, Gay—and not material things that were primary. They formed the basis of her memories. Children always place relationships above things.

Kids' Perceptions Depend on Prior Knowledge

Grown-ups too often forget this. Stephanie did not think about losing toys or other treasured belongings or the poor, doomed goldfish on her dresser. She may have been taught at some time or other that fires destroy property, but that was mere theory. It did not sink in until well after the fact that major destruction was occurring here. At the time she had no concept of the scope of the event because she had never experienced anything like that before.

Very often, particularly when it's an emotionally traumatic event, such as the death of a beloved friend or relative, parents expect their small children to think and behave in adult ways. I remember specifically a woman who was angry that her four-year-old son kept asking for Gramma months after Gramma passed away. "How many times have I told him Gramma's dead and gone to heaven?" the frazzled woman complained. "And he turns right around and asks it again. He drives me nuts!"

Her child did not grasp the reality of death. The child had no background knowledge or experience upon which to draw. Indeed, his grandmother's death *was* the experience upon which he would draw in the future. His mother's patience, as he came to grips with the hardest lesson of life, was crucial here.

Kids' Perceptions Change with Age

This point is a corollary of the prior knowledge point. As children mature and their background of general knowledge grows, their perceptions change. They react to new events in different ways as they mature, and they reprocess the past as well.

Stephanie was doing that reprocessing two years later. She was older now, riding her bike to the store, winning the spelling bee in her school, playing soccer in the park league. Her horizons had expanded far beyond the confines of her home. Now her mind was reprocessing her memories according to the new Stephanie, who was not at all like the seven year old who originally experienced the fire. Her grieving was more mature now, and there had been loss to grieve. Grief for a beloved Barbie doll? She hadn't even thought about that Barbie doll for years. But the loss had to be grieved again at Stephanie's level of understanding. She had to grieve the goldfish too.

Children's perceptions of the world change as well, and this affects their memories. Brand new babies don't pay much attention to anything in the world except that which is right in front of their face. Literally. As they grow, they learn to reach out and grasp things. Their world has expanded to what they can reach. Oh, certainly, an infant might see an elephant at the zoo, but the elephant doesn't mean anything. As the babies learn to crawl, their world of interest becomes the whole house.

Not until they start school will their world of interest extend beyond home and yard and immediate neighborhood into the greater neighborhood.

In later years Stephanie's little brother Chad will probably say, "The fire? I was too young to remember much about it." That will be true in a sense. His perceptions at that age were limited. But it will not mean that he was too young for the memory to stick. It sticks, all right. What sticks though is not a videotape of the event but his perceptions, based upon his five-year-old world. He didn't much notice things beyond Momma's arms—certainly not the fire in his house. Only because of those flashing lights and sirens did the fire trucks make an impression. The fire fighters did not; they were remote from his interest or experience. In a dozen different ways, he was seeing the event differently than did Stephanie or his parents or any of the onlookers.

How Kids' Memories Are Made

When the smoke alarm awakened her, Stephanie knew what to do. She knew to crawl, staying low. When her mother helped her out the window, she knew to run to an assigned meeting place, the mailbox at the curb. Although her mother reminded her anyway, she knew she must not under any circumstance go back inside the house. Daddy had not come out yet, but her job was to stand by the mailbox. Nothing else. How did she know all these things?

Implanting Skills in Memory

Her father wisely conducted fire drills a couple of times a year. I urge every parent to do the same. The child who knows just what to do in an emergency is not only safer but much less frightened and confused by the event.

Ron taught the children well by teaching more than one area of their memory—episodic and procedural. Simply telling the children what to do should an emergency arise would not have taught them anything. Stephanie and Chad were too young to hear instructions and follow them months, or perhaps years, later. So Ron taught their bodies as well as their heads.

Ron and his wife both demonstrated crawling around, dropping and rolling, and checking doors. They exited through a window or door in every room of the house, showing the kids what to do. That activity imprinted the lessons in the kids' episodic memory. Then they led the children through it all. The kids dropped and rolled. They crawled. They climbed out windows. Not just once, but many times. Over and over they ran out to stand by the mailbox on the curb. When they needed the skill their procedural memory immediately came into play. Children must have that procedural experience for a reason I can illustrate with a conversation I once overheard.

I listened to a woman tell another woman how to do something in knitting called "Slip one, knit one, PSSO." It is apparently a method of decreasing the number of stitches on the needles. The interesting part was that the lesson was given over the phone.

"All right, Beth. Slip the first stitch in the row from your left needle to the right one without drawing a yarn loop through. Straight across. Got it? Good. Now knit the second stitch in the regular way and stop." She paused a moment. "You have two stitches on your right-hand needle, right? Now use the tip of your left needle to drag the first stitch up and over the second one. That's all there is to it." Another pause. "Twisted, huh? Okay, go back to the beginning." Pause. "Now when you slip that first stitch, go into it from right to left. Straight across, not knitwise. Okay? Now knit the second stitch and pass the slipped stitch straight up over it." Pause. "Great!"

Success. The woman giving the instructions had no knitting needles in hand as she talked Beth through it. She closed her eyes and envisioned the process as if she were performing it herself, then described that mental image to Beth.

A small child cannot do that. The child cannot envision something from a description or describe something without actually doing it (assuming the child's verbal skills would be up to the task). The child has to physically do it and see it done. The smaller the child, the more important this becomes.

Often, usually during fire prevention week, fire fighters will visit the grade school, put on their bunker gear, and show the kids what a fire fighter looks like all dressed up. In full turnouts they're pretty frightening with the helmet and hood and the air pack on their back. They will activate the beeper that helps others locate them by sound because visibility in a burning structure is almost always zero. Then the kids practice running to the uniformed fire fighters. You see, a frightened child, especially a small child, will hide from that big, scary creature unless the lesson not to is planted deeply. A video won't plant it. Talking won't come close. By seeing and doing, the small child learns to overcome the natural, fatal tendency to hide.

Even adults benefit immensely from physically going through the motions of a skill. This is why medical technicians, first responders, and paramedics must review cardiopulmonary resuscitation techniques annually. They must practice the motions on life-sized dummies built specifically for that purpose. When the time comes to use the skills, they automatically do it right.

In fact, we're beginning to learn the value of older children and adults envisioning the performance of a skill. For example, batting practice. You can get out there on the field and hit balls over and over. That's excellent practice. But we are finding out that you can also improve your performance by envisioning yourself batting. As you mentally go through the motions, your brain practices sending the appropriate signals to your muscles.

That fascinates me. Your procedural memory calls up an activity—in this case, batting—and actually reinforces itself.

Children both learn and reinforce learning by this means. Often it takes the form of planning. You will remember several chapters back when Chad Houser was daydreaming about what color to paint his Housermobile? In an important sense, he was learning about painting, even rehearsing somewhat the process of painting, as he daydreamed.

When do kids' memories kick in so that you can start teaching them about their world? Prenatally. And that amazes me too.

How Early Do You Start?

I read a while back about the challenge a deaf man and his deaf wife had to meet when they gave birth to a child with normal hearing. Neither adult could speak clearly. The child, therefore, was not able to hear the parents speak, which is how children pick up the language, even from before birth. But they began teaching the child signed English (which is somewhat different from American sign language) from the very beginning.

At the age of three months the child used the sign for "milk." It was not a random gesture or an anomaly or a fond wish on the parents' part. The child was conveying wants through physical gesture that early.

Research shows that the number one effect that determines how an infant eventually turns out is how the mother loves the baby in the beginning. What is her attitude toward the child? That love, or lack of it, is encoded from birth on. Also encoded in the very earliest memory is the relationship between Mommy and Daddy. Children know that? Yes, they do, from the first moment.

Teaching therefore begins from birth and even before. That is when memories, as well as the memory process, are being generated and shaped.

Teaching Other Lessons to Children

When Stephanie went to school the day following the fire, she was amazed at how much fuss the teachers paid her. Two of the room mothers came in with donated clothing for her and Chad. It felt kind of like one of those Christmases when you get more clothes than toys—nice, but nothing to get excited about. Mommy came in and thanked the teacher and talked to her a while and helped the Bluebirds—the kids in the first two rows—with arithmetic.

They were using little wooden counting sticks in arithmetic for rapid adding and subtracting. A green stick was twice as long as a yellow one. You added two yellow ones to get a green one and two green ones plus a yellow one made a blue one. Stephanie was adept at manipulating red and purple ones too. She loved adding and taking away the sticks on her desk as she spouted out the answers to questions like "How much are seven and eleven?" In fact, she had most of the answers memorized by now. She didn't need the sticks.

Her little brother Chad, in kindergarten, would be even more dependent upon a physical aid to thinking. A child that age cannot picture abstracts well. Set out apples and the child can count apples. Write a number on the blackboard and the three year old can't make the connection. The five year old can, but he still needs the apples as well.

Before the age of three, neither child was any whiz at memorizing. Hardly any small child is. The ability to build and use memory grows with age as common pathways develop.

To teach a small child abstracts, the time-honored way is to use numerous pathways, such as auditory *and* visual *and* motor (that is, movement) paths. You are building memories in several different areas at once. As they interconnect, they support each other.

Chad learned cute songs. He drove Mommy nuts when he

would sing "Twinkle Twinkle Little Star" three dozen times in succession. (Did I mention that small children can't stay on key?) Stephanie's aunt taught her "I'm a Little Teapot," and she never missed an opportunity to sing it for guests. She loved the limelight.

Incidentally, how did her aunt teach her? By singing it (auditory), showing her the motions (visual), and manipulating and shaping her arms and body in the appropriate poses (motor).

And the "Alphabet Song"? To the tune of "Twinkle Twinkle Little Star," you sing the letters. How many of us learned our alphabet that way? And how many of us still catch ourselves singing it now and then as we're trying to file things alphabetically and rapidly?

Spoken language and sung language—the words of songs—follow different pathways. Chad and Stephanie learned their ABC's early and well because of that fact. Probably, so did you. By accessing long-term memory from the two different pathways, spoken and sung, the lesson stuck quicker and better.

This is one reason that I am so enthusiastic about singing around the campfire when my family and I go over to our ranch. It implants memories through a variety of pathways. Sitting around a fire at night is primal. Shepherds did it in the Holy Land thousands of years ago. Indians, cowboys, pioneers, and so many others have done it. It strikes a chord of togetherness that nothing else can. And singing the old time gospel songs implants messages and truths as no other teaching method can. "I am redeemed." Wonderful message. The most profound message we teach small children in a song is "Jesus loves me, this I know for the Bible tells me so."

I am somewhat aware how much the songs I grew up with shaped my faith and my attitudes today. I love them. That's why I want to pass them on to my children.

Teaching through more than one avenue is not just a device

to pump more information into small children. It also is a window with which to see into them.

Says Dr. Paul Warren, behavioral pediatrician at the Minirth Meier New Life Clinic, "I find it clinically interesting to watch kids in the act of memorizing. It tells you a lot about the children. You get a picture of how their emotions are developing as they win some and lose some with their memorizing. Do they get frustrated quickly? Are they dogged in their determination? Easily confused or distracted? You can also analyze their learning style by monitoring memorization. If they don't do well with long-term memorization, you know to give them other ways of learning besides memorization."

Other ways might include computers, calculators, hands-on training of some sort, or some wacky system you devise for a unique child.

A friend named Tom echoes that sentiment. He has been teaching math for several decades now, and his specialty is remedial math. The kids he gets in his large junior high school are not learning disabled as such, but they're usually labeled slow learners. "If a kid hasn't memorized the multiplication tables inside out by eighth grade, the child never will. Period. It's that simple. When I started handing out calculators in my seventh grade classes, I got all kinds of flak. The experts were telling me that calculators are a crutch. The kid will never learn to walk if you give him a crutch. That was the philosophy then. Browbeat them into learning those tables."

Tom shakes his head. "No. That's not true. These kids just aren't capable of getting it through the usual teaching channels. They'll drop out. They'll struggle through school feeling like losers, but they won't blot up a lot of memorized numbers, no matter how much some adult pushes them. Their memories simply aren't wired that way. They're not stupid. They're different. A calculator is not their crutch. It's their wings."

Minimizing Bad Memories in Children

Only one kind of teaching involves the absorption of math or language material—what we lump together as "school." Another is teaching emotions. Can emotions be learned? Oh, yes! But you don't teach them the way you teach the alphabet.

None of us can prevent our little ones from having bad memories because they are a part of real life. Bad things happen. The best we can do is minimize the harm and derive a good lesson the child can use in the future.

Let's say, for example, that the house fire occurred not when Stephanie was seven, but when she was eleven. By that age she had a pretty good grasp of what danger and tragedy are, and she was experienced enough with other losses in life that she could realize how great a loss the fire inflicted. She knew about death, if not in fact, at least in theory.

While her father delayed leaving the house, she agonized. It's not exaggerating to say she was terrified for his safety. Unlike the younger Stephanie, she experienced immense shame and frustration at being able to do nothing heroic to stop the fire and remedy the whole horrible situation. An eleven year old is beginning to feel the I-can-do-anything invincibility of the teen years. What could Ron and his wife have done to help their daughter at that age?

The same things they could do for the younger Stephanie and Chad.

Three healthy impressions mark good memories even in bad situations: tender touching, open communication, and a sense of security.

Tender Touching

The hug, the squeeze. Stephanie yearned for a hug at age seven, and she would have accepted one just as gladly at age eleven. Most adults would too. Whether or not the child later remembers specifically being hugged and snuggled, the child will recall the warm, positive emotion associated with it.

A tender, loving touch says, "You are loved; you are safe," in nonverbal terms the smallest baby understands. We are born understanding the touch of another human being.

Open Communication

Ron communicated quite openly when he threw his useless phone into the hydrangea. It's not a thing Stephanie wanted or needed to "hear," but people in their anger and frustration do things like that. Ron could have eased the seven year old's mind, and even more so the eleven year old's, by talking about it afterward. "I was angry! I had forgotten the thing needed a new battery, and I was so frustrated! And scared. I know what a fire can do." Simply by openly acknowledging his own feelings, he can validate the child's feelings:

"I shouldn't have done that."

"I'm angry because you did such and so."

"I'm so proud of you!"

"I watch you come out in the kitchen in the morning and I thank God for you. You're so special."

The communications themselves are actually secondary in all this. The child may not be able to bring back to conscious memory the words you said. That doesn't matter. The child retains the feelings. You can tell a kid she's no good, and that message may not reach her conscious mind again. But the feeling *I'm no good* will not be forgotten. Primary in open communication, then, is the feeling expressed and the sincerity.

A Sense of Security

I am convinced that one of the most important feelings a child can have growing up is to feel safe. It is second only to feeling loved.

Even as her world was tumbling down around her, seven-year-old Stephanie felt safe. Her mommy was there. Stephanie herself knew what she must do. She was loved, and she would not be abandoned.

Oh, sure, it was scary standing out in the cold darkness on the curb, waiting for Daddy, waiting for Mommy to return from calling in the fire, feeling her little brother clinging and shaking. But Stephanie *knew* that part would pass quickly. Mommy wouldn't leave her alone long. Daddy would come.

Had Stephanie not had that assurance, the experience would have been far more traumatic for her.

Unfortunately, many children lack a feeling of security. While these feelings do not press upon their conscious mind day by day, they do stick in the memory. Remember that children's emotions emerge into recall even when the episodes do not. Several things can destroy feelings of security.

Being forced to make adult decisions

When children are out of their league, so to speak, they feel insecure. So do you when you have to face a task for which you're unprepared. I'm thinking just now of families I knew when I was growing up in Arkansas. Children eleven or twelve years old would be left for a few hours with the care of younger brothers and sisters. Now all that's fine as long as everything is rolling along normally. But should an emergency occur, the child in charge is faced with some terrifying decisions that must be made instantly. Almost never is that child trained or prepared to make them. That's not only frightening, it's exceedingly dangerous. Should the child make a wrong decision, the consequences could remain for life. "If only I had done so-and-so." That's so sad! Even if the outcome is favorable, perhaps heroic, the fear and insecurity of having to make the decisions haunt the memory.

Having heavier responsibilities than is appropriate

In the families I just mentioned, if the little ones got into trouble, the older child got the blame. How many times I would hear the neighbor lady scold her ten-year-old daughter with, "Missy, there's your little sister in the mud again! I told you to watch her!" The truth is, many adults are hard-pressed to keep kids properly lined up and marching right. Children under the age of twelve certainly get no respect from little ones.

When Mommy asked Stephanie to go out the window first and help her brother, Stephanie was given a single task to do under Mommy's immediate supervision. She was helping an adult, not shouldering an adult responsibility. When she failed at first to awaken Chad, Elaine did not hold her responsible. She did what she was supposed to and was not held accountable for more. Would Stephanie ponder all these ramifications at conscious level? Of course not. Were they entering and shaping her memory of the incident below conscious level? You bet.

Having to cope alone

Children in two-parent families with an adult around at all times may have to cope with life on their own just the same as the latchkey kid. If the adults are not emotionally and psychologically available, the child must face life essentially alone.

The daughter of an acquaintance witnessed a fatal drive-by shooting. You hear about such things, but you never think much about them. They certainly never happen nearby. But this one occurred right in front of her. She watched a young man die at the entrance of a shopping mall. She knew the boy.

Some months afterward I asked the acquaintance how his daughter was doing. He seemed surprised by my question. "Fine, I guess. Okay. Why would she be doing badly?"

I said that the scene she had witnessed was too intense to simply slide by. Did she talk about it much? Give any indication of her feelings?

"Oh, that. That was months ago." He shrugged. "I never asked her."

In the midst of a supposedly close, happy, intact family, that girl was carrying an onerous burden alone.

Maximizing the Good in Bad Memories

To mend bad memories—in effect to put the best possible spin on a disastrous situation—you want to reverse the items I just discussed above. They work both ways. Those insecurity-builders are what make bad memories worse. To make bad memories better, see that the opposite happens.

For starters, make certain those three aspects—touching, communicating, and offering security—are a part of the memory. Ron could have eased his children's terror greatly had he paused to give them a hug. A quick hug is better than no hug. His wife held them; that is better yet. In any bad situation, hug if you can. Add appropriate touching to any verbal reassurance.

Keep communication open. When the child expresses a negative emotion, such as, "I'm scared, Daddy!" Daddy never wants to come back with, "You're not *really* scared." Do you see the problem that can cause? Daddy just negated his child's feeling. In his desire to minimize the frightened feeling, he essentially told the child she was lying. His child can express feelings again sometime, with the fear that they will be denied again, or the child can simply not communicate the feelings. The child will often bottle them up to avoid hearing that the expressed emotion is false or wrong.

Ron could either respond to his children's declaration—"I'm scared," or "This is exciting!"—with a simple "You bet!" or "I believe it." Even better, he could volunteer something on the order of, "This must be scary for you." Or "I think this is exciting. Do you?"

A sense of security does not come instantly to the scene, the way a touch or a word does. Certainly, having Mommy there and seeing that she was attentive made the kids feel safe. But their real security lay in knowing through repeated prior experience that Mommy and Daddy would take care of the matter. They knew they would not be called upon to do more than they were trained for or capable of. Moreover, they were thoroughly trained to respond at their level in the emergency. All this added up to a deeply abiding sense of security.

Do your children and your children's friends have the training and preparation to respond to most basic emergencies? Are the skills and duties they are called upon to perform commensurate with their age? Do they know you will be there?

This brings us to one final way in which you can make the best of bad memories: modeling.

Be the Kind of Memory You Want to Have

Two weeks after he got his driver's license, the sixteen-year-old son of an associate, a single mother, rolled his car. It happened in an instant as he was groping under the seat for a music cassette. Driving at normal speed westbound, he drifted right, his tires caught in the gravel, he oversteered, and his swerve sent the car across the road into the opposite ditch, rolling it from wheels to roof to wheels. It came to rest in a cow pasture, facing eastbound.

His mom had gone to work (fifty mile commute one way) two hours earlier, and he and his two friends were driving to school. They all had their seatbelts buckled. They all emerged unscathed. To say they were disoriented and upset is understating it.

The first thing this teenager did was call his mom. She gave him the numbers of their hospitalization policy and told him to get everyone checked out. She gave him clear directions, which he wrote down. She might have been fifty miles away, but he was not alone. Her voice was firm, steady, and authoritative. She did not criticize or scold. She praised his good sense to have buckled up, and she expressed her love and relief.

His mom modeled the kind of response she wanted her son to have as an adult. She taught him more that morning than all the driver's education courses in the world could. Ten years later he still clearly remembered flying end over end; he still remembered watching the tow truck haul away his lovely little car. But most of all he remembered Mom's solid, loving support, even though she was nowhere near.

What he did not know until ten years later was that as soon as she hung up the phone she fell apart!

Did Ron blow the modeling bit when he let anger and frustration get the better of him the night of the fire? No. People do not always make the best possible response, particularly in an emergency. He could, however, have imparted a valuable lesson during subsequent conversations with his children had he admitted his response was less than perfect. Then he would be showing them that we make mistakes and can rise above them. In normal family situations the Lord can cover a lot of mistakes. "My grace is sufficient for you," He said (2 Cor. 12:9). Bad attitudes and neglect hurt kids. Mistakes don't hurt kids.

By the time they reach their teen years, Ron's children will see Mommy and Daddy make errors, and they will also observe them rise above their situation brilliantly. They will see the gamut of human strength and frailty. And all the while, their memories, often below conscious level, will be recording these lessons on how to respond.

Let's look at the special world of teens next.

11

Shaping Teen Memories

During one of his last appearances on New Year's Eve, as his band was about to play "Auld Lang Syne" yet again, Guy Lombardo consented to an interview. A television camera recorded it. At one point the renowned bandleader told about "dippers" back in the thirties and forties. "They were the couples—teens mostly—who would dance their way to a dark corner of the floor and do a deep dip. While they were down, they'd kiss." As he said this, the camera showed an old man who was listening to the interview. You could tell he was once a dipper; he was nodding quietly as tears streamed down his face.

Teen memories. Half a century later they burn as brightly as ever. A teenager is wise and foolish, careless and intensely idealistic, grabbing life at its fullest and shrinking back in fear. Injustice hurts more. Outrage bites deeper. At no other time in a person's life, except for the first six months after birth, does a person change so rapidly in so many ways. Never again will that person live so intensely moment by moment. The teen years are also years of acute loss. Adults forget that too often. Teenagers have to give up childhood, assume responsibilities they did not know as kids, watch the very luxury of being a kid slip away. It is wise to nurture teens' memories, promoting good ones and minimizing bad ones, because they last so long and shape so effectively.

Even more important, reading and managing memories is the best way to keep communication with teens during those important and frustrating breakaway years, as kids forcibly evict themselves from the nest, psychologically as well as residentially. It is a special time with special problems, and you can make the best of it by paying attention to memories, both those from the past and those made today for the future.

Getting a Read on the Past

Reading a teen's memories is the fastest way to learn what the teen is thinking.

"I don't want to know what she's thinking," a woman we will call Lorraine protested. "I already have a pretty good idea what she's thinking. I want to know how to keep her from getting pregnant."

Lorraine's story is worth pursuing because it provides a good example of how memories influence the challenges and opportunities of raising teens.

The "she" to whom Lorraine referred was her daughter, Kristin. Kristin, fifteen, was one of those brilliant kids who earns, at best, so-so grades. Lorraine claimed she was lazy scholastically. Kristin did not excel in sports. She did not excel in crafts or art. She attended school athletic events, not to cheer the team on but to see who else was there. Kristin fit in well with her peer group, a gaggle of noisy kids the neighbors would sniff about and point to as they said, "You see? Today's kids are absolutely worthless!"

Lorraine and her husband, Gerrald, sought counseling as a last resort. Not only were they petrified about Kristin's low grades and fast lifestyle, they were afraid Kristin's problems, unsolved, would spread to her two younger siblings, an eleven-year-old boy and a ten-year-old girl.

Kristin sat in this first session sour-faced with her arms tightly crossed. Kristin was not going to be an easy interviewee. If you were conversing with a teen like Kristin, what would you look for as clues to her inner thoughts? For that matter, why should you want to, and what has that to do with memory? First, you must know what is going on in her thoughts if you are to understand her and help her meet life well. Everything going on in her thoughts is based on her memories, both the ones that readily come to her mind and the ones hidden. Second, a large part of helping any child, teens included, is to reshape memories that need reshaping. That means knowing what's there. The first and best way to read and know what's there is simply to spend time with him or her.

Spend the Time

"Don't tell me I have to talk to her," Gerrald complained. "We must have sat at the kitchen table for half an hour last night, and she just wouldn't open up. It's like trying to draw conversation out of a brick. I'd ask her a question, and she'd give me a grunt for an answer. Drove me nuts! I'm not going to waste my time again until she decides to cooperate."

Half an hour? Sitting there? Gerrald's relationship with his daughter had never been very close. It's no wonder half an hour wouldn't do it, and grilling her with questions didn't do it either. To make conversational contact with Kristin, you might consider taking her to a movie or athletic event. You would take her out for a snack afterward—pizza, frozen yogurt, fast food, or something. You would converse. Not interrogate. Chat.

When Gerrald attempted this with Kristin, it didn't work at first. Usually, Kristin trooped off with a bevy of friends after events. She resented having instead to go out for pizza with her stuffy old dad.

Gerrald persisted, though, and he learned eventually that he had to hang out with Kristin, attending some event or activity, for a minimum of an hour before she started to really get to deep issues. Sheer time in the saddle is what it took.

Lorraine learned something else significant about time; Kristin's golden hours extended between 11 P.M. and 2 A.M. Very late at night the defenses came down. When she came in from some group activity or event, she and Lorraine could sit around the table with hot chocolate and talk.

A good time to talk with your child is when you are driving from place to place in the car. But make sure the radio is off. A nonpersonal distraction for both, such as attention paid to the road ahead, sometimes greases the skids of a conversation and helps it move more smoothly.

To open communication, then, choose an appropriate time. This will be at the teen's best time, not at your convenience. As you talk, look for clues to what's really going on inside, such as throwaway lines and gestures.

Throwaway Lines

Kids are like the cherry trees along the Tidal Basin in Washington, D.C. If you want to see them bloom, you have to be there during the two weeks they are blooming. The other fifty weeks you can visit as avidly as you wish without seeing a single blossom. With teenagers you have to catch the right word at the right moment. It won't spill into your lap just any old time.

Teens are easily hurt and instinctively guard their feelings, putting up careful defenses. One of these protective defenses is to simply avoid discussing topics about which they feel vulnerable. As a result, kids don't talk about what they are thinking (neither do grown-ups, but that's another matter). It's such a strong protective mechanism that they don't always know they are not talking about what they're thinking. For one reason or another, then, they skate all around the rink without ever getting to the center. But it will come out, given time. Time is the key.

Because of this powerful feeling of vulnerability, kids drop their most significant tidbits as little throwaway lines, and you have to be there to catch them. Another guideline both Gerrald and Lorraine could follow then, would be to listen to everything. Certainly, hear the high spots and the major points. But listen to the little goodies as well.

Kristin, for example, was talking about the girls from her homeroom who had just made the cheerleading team. "Rachel's the worst," she explained. "Rachel was born with a hairbrush in her hand. She's constantly primping, and I do mean constantly. I wonder if she'd be that bad if she had mousey old hair like mine instead of strawberry blonde. And Genelle. She has that short haircut that frames her face just right. Gorgeous, and she never has to try. But Pat and Laura . . ."

Did you catch it? Kristin's self-esteem was in the dumps and probably her spirits as well. Her casual comment about her hair was the tip-off. Lorraine would be wise to start listening for other self-deprecating remarks.

Where did that measure of esteem (or lack of it) come from? From the great stack of memories she accumulated, every one of which she weighed against her own self-worth. Should an acquaintance casually mention that she doesn't like blue eye shadow, and Kristin does, the teen will immediately assume that her taste is less refined than that acquaintance's, and it's a comment about her personally. No matter that Kristin had never worn eye shadow or that the acquaintance's opinion means nothing. That's how pervasively her memories color her attitudes, toward herself in particular and also toward others.

Gestures are another way to read between the lines of a teenager's personality.

Gestures and Body Language

"Kristin flops around like a fish on a flat rock," Gerrald said. "Her hands are constantly flying when she talks."

What would you look for if you were watching a teen like Kristin? As a general rule, gestures held tight and close to the body indicate nervousness, perhaps an angry or uptight attitude. With her pouting lower lip out and her arms crossed, Kristin told the world, "This is not my idea, and I don't like it."

Gestures moving up and away from the body suggest just the opposite—an open, outgoing attitude. On one occasion as she described a slumber party at a friend's house, she swept her arms up and out in an expansive swoop. It was a very positive and upbeat thing to do.

Perhaps you don't "know" what various gestures and movements indicate. As you learn to read your teens well, observe and analyze. Consider their interests. For instance, boys and girls with a strong interest in some sport might use referees' gestures, such as time out. Watching the kid "flop around," ask yourself, "If I were making that gesture or movement, how would I be feeling?" Gestures are amazingly universal.

I have found that very often kids' words and their gestures say different things. Sometimes those things are poles apart. Often, I "hear" the gestures speaking more loudly than the words, and I believe the gestures. When a teen says, "I feel fine. No problem," as he keeps his arms and legs tucked in close and his eyes downcast, his gestures are saying, "I'm so depressed I can't stand myself."

In fact, I'll just about always go with the gestures. Kids often say what they want you to know or what they think you want to hear rather than the unvarnished truth. Spontaneous gestures and body language, however, are very hard to control. Kids' body language rarely lies. But that, you see, is a clue in itself. In the case of the boy who claimed he was feeling fine, I would discern that he was so fearful about his depression or sadness that he carefully and vehemently denied it to himself and others.

Now, you've gathered your basic information—the raw

data—the conversation itself and your perceptions derived from it. But that's not the end; it's the beginning. Now you must weigh what you have seen and heard from your teen.

Consider What You've Received

Spend some time reflecting on the conversation you have just had with your kid.

What was the tone when the conversation began, and what was the tone at its end? Were you and your teen animated? Sullen? Angry? What happened next? For one thing, you'll see whether your talks are progressing. If the tone improves, you're probably (but not always!) making a good connection.

Assume for the moment that the kid is trying to hide something. What did you not discuss? Did you bowl into some subject only to have the child bowl right back out? Did you detect reticence? Shame? Anger? Some unexpected reaction?

How did your teen's statements, throwaways, and attitudes differ from what you perceive to be reality? For example, Lorraine picked up, mostly through nuances and hints, that Kristin really did not like herself. She did not like the way she looked or the way she acted. She didn't consider herself as good as other girls her age, and she felt she was less desirable to boys.

Lorraine quite properly carried that observation to a frightening conclusion. In her desire to be accepted, might Kristin go further faster with boys than would a girl who was self-confident and more secure? Listening between the lines of her daughter's monologues, Lorraine became more and more convinced the answer was yes. How would she tackle this revelation? For that matter how would she determine if her supposition were valid? Here's where memories can help.

How Do Memories Relate to What You Hear?

"Memories?" Lorraine smiled. "When I was seven—and this was way back when—my aunt and uncle brought me along from New Jersey to Ohio. I had a baby rabbit with us, traveling in a little wooden crate. When I talked to my uncle years afterward, he complained about the lousy motel cabin accommodations. At one place we slept on the floor. I don't remember any of that. I remember only my aunt and uncle and the rabbit."

Adults remember circumstances and situations. Kids remember relationships. Lorraine recalled the rabbit and her aunt and uncle—the relationships. She didn't remember sleeping on the floor. Kids adjust instantly to things like that. What would your children remember about incidents in your own memory?

Over time you can get a fairly good handle on your children's memories. Listen, keeping in mind that their memories will be of relationships and possibly of places, *if* the places possess an emotional significance. Although you know a lot about your teens' memories, you still know very little. Ask yourself, therefore, how the memories you know about might have colored the kids' perceptions.

The best way to go about answering that question is to get into reminiscence marathons. Usually, kids love to talk about the past. That is one area in which they can talk on a level with grown-ups. They may not have nearly as much past as Mom and Dad, but they have it, and it is unique for them.

You can start a reminiscence marathon with a simple, "That reminds me. Do you remember . . . ?" And one thing leads to another.

Gerrald got off work early one afternoon and sat with Kristin at her little brother's soccer match. "Hey, Sugar, look at the guy across the way with the pink ball cap. You remember that pink hat you wore when you were little? We couldn't get it off you."

Kristin chilled instantly. A month ago Gerrald wouldn't have noticed. But he was paying better attention to her now.

He pushed a little. "You wore it in kindergarten, as I recall."

"Yeah."

"So why'd you quit?"

"Mrs. Garvey laughed at it."

Gerrald learned a lot by fleshing out that careless little line with what he already knew. He knew that Kristin had idolized her kindergarten teacher, Mrs. Garvey. He knew that Kristin's passion for wearing her pink hat stopped, but he now remembered it had stopped abruptly. And a decade later, Kristin still remembered.

"What did she say?" Gerrald asked.

Kristin shrugged mightily (overblown gestures indicate extreme feelings; great joy, great anger, great sadness). "She thought it was stupid, and it made me ugly."

"She's a nice lady. How could she be so wrong?"

Gerrald left it there, but the exchange haunted him. The next day he called up Mrs. Garvey. He had to go through the school to reach her; she'd been retired a couple of years. Their conversation went like this:

Gerrald: "I don't know if you remember my daughter Kristin. Blond, active."

Mrs. Garvey: "Oh, my, yes! Such a pretty, personable little girl. Even then she had a way that was all her own. A uniqueness."

Gerrald: "Do you remember a pink hat she used to wear all the time?"

Mrs. Garvey: "I certainly do. I got pretty tired of her constantly wearing it. She refused to take if off. I made her remove it during class, of course. But the moment recess began or we went outside, there it was. It was a cute little hat, and she looked just darling in it."

Gerrald: "Oh? She feels that you thought it was ugly."

Mrs. Garvey: "Oh, no. That's just what I had to tell her in order to get her to leave it home."

Gerrald ended the conversation quickly because rage was boiling up inside him. Of all people, Mrs. Garvey, the veteran kindergarten teacher, must know that when a child is five, teachers are gods. Whatever she said, Kristin would believe. But she disparaged the hat, a thing Kristin held very dear, for no other reason than that it apparently irritated her. It was a harmless thing she happened to find annoying, and she lied to the little girl. Worse yet, she maligned Kristin herself. *Ugly* is an incredibly ugly word to a five-year-old.

Very often I find that a child has adopted some casual statement or criticism, however unmerited it may be, as a life-shaping definition. Whether the child does so consciously or not, that memory lasts forever at some level. Put a few false, careless statements together, and the child's perspective can be totally altered for the worse.

Gerrald planned to talk about it with Kristin that evening. Mrs. Garvey's casual little statement had bothered Kristin enough that she remembered it ten years later. And it was unwarranted. Pretty and vivacious, Kristin suffered a very low self-image. Whether Mrs. Garvey's comment was the source of that poor self-image or merely one drop in a bucket of such memories, it hurt Kristin. He picked up the phone again.

It took him almost five minutes to reach Kristin at school, have her called away from gym class, and get her on the line.

She picked up the receiver in a panic. "What happened, Dad? What's wrong?"

"Everyone's fine, Sugar. Nothing's wrong that way. It's just that I'm so furious I can't stand it, and I had to call you." He explained the conversation he'd just had with Mrs. Garvey, quoting word for word. He ended with, "We can talk more tonight. I'm so mad I can't see straight. I had to get this off my chest is all."

I don't advocate casually disrupting a child's school day, not even when it's gym class. But in this case his intense anger meant more to her than ten thousand carefully framed and considered words. He was concerned enough to spend considerable effort tracking the matter down. That can impress a teenager. Teenagers burn. He burned. They act impulsively. He acted impulsively and from a caring heart.

Late that night, as they mulled Mrs. Garvey's little ploy and how it might still be coloring Kristin's whole view of herself, father and daughter talked heart to heart at the deepest level for nearly the first time. Most important of all, Kristin began to see herself differently as Mrs. Garvey's words took on a different cast.

Her father could not erase that memory. He could not change the past. But now that she was older, Kristin was able to recall that memory in a different light. It was not a solution in itself, but it was an excellent start on the solution to Kristin's poor self view.

There are other ways in which memories play a major part in teen-parent relationships. One of them is the warping memory inside the adult.

Using Our Memories to Help a Child

Said one lad grandiloquently, "Parents? They weren't born, they were hatched. They had to be. They don't have the foggiest idea what we're going through." Parents, most kids believe, suffer premature onset of Alzheimer's the moment the kids turn thirteen. Conversely, rock music has appealed to kids since its inception because it conveys the message, "We feel like you do. We have the same questions." Kids think modern music understands. Parents? Hmph. Parents, the kids think, cannot remember what it was like to be a teenager.

Know what? In a large way they're right. How often do adults, weighed down by responsibility, either imply or say outright, "You have it easy. Your problems are nothing. You don't know how good you've got it now." Is it true that teens have an easier time than their parents?

We asked a group of adults, all parents of kids still at home, about their own teen years. Most remembered very little of their lives outside school. Eighty percent of the adults we quizzed came up with primarily bad memories of their own teenage years.

I think this underscores the turmoil of teens' lives—all teens—and it's not getting any better. Under the best of circumstances adolescence is painful, and rare indeed is the teenager who grows up under the best of circumstances. But it's exciting, too, to be transformed from child to adult, ready or not. It's adventurous to be ripping away from the past. But it hurts as well, and any dysfunction in the family multiplies the pain. It's not something your mind likes to dwell upon.

It's almost a standing joke that every father is suspicious of every boy his daughter dates because he was young himself once and he knows what it's like to be hormone impaired. He's sure he knows exactly what that boy is thinking.

"Most parents," Dr. Paul Warren, behavioral pediatrician, sums up, "possess either negative memories or no memories at all about what it's like to be a teen. Without that empathy, it's hard to be the parent of an adolescent."

The flip side is just as true. Memories are such an integral part of us that whatever our own memories of adolescence might be, they will profoundly effect how we parent teens. As Paul says, "You learn to be a parent by being a kid first. You learn to be an adult by being a kid first."

When dealing with your emerging adult, you can use memories in several ways.

Empathy from Memories

"So you've been riding Kristin pretty hard about keeping schoolwork up," their counselor prompted.

Lorraine bobbed her head. "It's so important, and she's just plain being lazy. She could do very well in school if she'd only apply herself better."

Gerrald agreed. "It's not one of these things you read about where the parents live their lives vicariously through their kids, so they want the kids to excel. It's for her. She needs the edge good grades will give her in life, especially since she's mentally capable of earning that edge."

"What were your grades like?"

The conversation thudded to a near halt. Lorraine and Gerrald both carried a lackluster academic performance from high school right through college. Neither made the dean's list. Neither was voted most likely to succeed at anything.

"Oh, wow!" was Kristin's wide-eyed response to that revelation. "The way they talked, I was sure they were both four-pointers!"

At any stage of life, grades aren't important. Relationships are. As Lorraine and Gerrald started reminiscing about their own struggles with grades, two things happened. Their frustration with Kristin softened. They lifted some of the pressure, a good move because the pressure they had been applying hadn't done a thing except alienate her, and Kristin saw her parents in a new and more generous light. She could relate to them better, seeing that they had faced the same struggles and frustrations.

Another way to use memories is as an indicator of the future.

Prophetic Nature of Memories

Here again is where Lorraine and Gerrald had not been quite up-front with Kristin. At sixteen Lorraine bore a child out of wedlock and gave it up for adoption. She met Gerrald two years later, and they married at age twenty. She told him about the baby before their wedding, and they pretty much came to terms with it. When Kristin arrived the incident was ancient history and never brought up.

"I am petrified," Lorraine whispered hoarsely, "that the same thing will happen to Kristin. That she'll have to go through that. Just petrified. You can't imagine how . . ." and her voice cracked.

Psychiatrists and other counselors uncover this source of pure terror over and over and over as they talk with parents: The parents develop an almost pathological fear that their child will make a mistake they also made. So they bury the mistake, whatever it is. They refuse to let it surface for fear the child will somehow eagerly run out and recreate it.

Would the kids do that, really? Quite possibly. Adults don't realize (and usually, neither do the kids), that when they hide powerful realities, they are placing indelible attitudes and thoughts in the darkest corners of their children's minds. Kids are incredibly sensitive in picking up that sort of thing below conscious level. Lorraine and Gerrald did not know that with their shame-based hidden memories they were programming Kristin's thinking in subtle, dangerous ways.

When fear such as Lorraine's—that Kristin would make the same mistake Lorraine made—becomes too intense, too tyrannical, the parent sometimes transfers the fear itself directly to the child. Because the mistake was buried, Lorraine and Gerrald weren't doing any programming at a conscious level. It was going on in subtle ways we are only now beginning to understand. In effect, Lorraine was programming Kristin to fear the same possibility even though Kristin had no idea exactly what the possible situation was.

"But isn't that good?" Lorraine asked.

Not necessarily. That sort of programming sets the child up to explore and find out what the unspoken fear is all about. Forbidden fruit is delectable. (This, incidentally, is one of the reasons why mystery fiction has been popular for so long. There is in the human heart the tantalizing desire to ferret out a secret. The Hardy Boys and Nancy Drew couldn't leave a mysterious clue unexamined. This sort of curiosity is compelling to a child.)

Lorraine and Gerrald had to work out a balance. On one side of the seesaw they had to warn their child against repeating Lorraine's mistake. On the other end, they had to limit the fear tactics both spoken and unspoken that would drive the girl to greater risk.

"So now what do we do?" Lorraine said, staring at Gerrald, crestfallen.

Gerrald stared at Lorraine. "I don't know. Honesty?"

"Tell her? I can't! No. Something else."

Lorraine was intuitively correct that they ought to do something. She was now aware that her adolescence could very likely prophesy Kristin's. And she felt paralyzed. The memories of her own pain and shame and sadness came flooding back as she thought about the link between her past and her daughter's. And the more they returned, the less she could talk about them.

Can secrets be buried forever? Possibly. But for practical purposes, especially within a family, I would have to say no.

As an example of a secret surfacing years after the fact, I think of the sister of a friend. Let's call her Michelle. Michelle from the age of twenty on was involved with a married man. He was the light of her life. Her mother virtually disowned her. Michelle became a Christian and turned away from the sin as best she could. Even so, it took her nearly three years to end the affair, and she ached for the man for years thereafter.

Michelle was fifty-one when her eighty-year-old mother died. Sorting through the material record of Mom's lifetime, Michelle and her brother came across a motel business card tucked away in the recesses of Mom's wallet—an old, old card from back before zip codes and seven-digit phone numbers. In their father's handwriting it was inscribed, "I'll string along with you."

"I'll String Along with You" was an immensely popular song of the thirties. Their mom's favorite, as they recalled. The title was the last line. The first line? "You may not be an angel, for angels are so few. . . ."

Digging deeper, Michelle learned from an elderly cousin that her mother was an adulteress and home wrecker, taking her father away from his first marriage. The new couple moved to a different state and led an exemplary life as pillars of the community. Michelle's father served on the school board, on the town council, in his fraternal order. Her mother had never offered a hint of her past. The motel business card remained hidden for over fifty years. But her past was replayed anyway.

Powerful forces were at work in Lorraine's family because of her secret. They could be working in yours.

Getting Past the Past

Lorraine had to first accept that she must resolve her own teenage past or she would inflict it on her teenager. Reasoning that, "If this business were really taken care of, I'd at least be able to talk about it," she decided on counsel to help her work through her pain and bad memories. "Maybe I could do it on my own, given some time," she said. "But we don't have any time. I have to do it now and do it quickly. Kristin is midway through her teens already. I can't afford to wait."

Then she took a big step. She told Kristin what she was doing and why. No longer was it a case of Mom preaching to the daughter to be good. It had become a lesson by example. Many years after her mistake Lorraine was still suffering. All the preaching in the world could not speak to Kristin the way Lorraine's struggle did. "This was the mistake; it was wrong. These are some of the consequences. I love you, Kristin, and I would spare you this."

Lorraine and her daughter illustrate another important point about memories. They are cause for hope.

Lorraine's neighbors loved to bad-mouth teenagers in general and Kristin's canty bunch of friends in particular. As Lorraine put it, "Sure, they're not the most exemplary kids in the world. They're noisy and thoughtless and disrespectful and a few other things. If I had my choice, Kristin would be running around with the top SAT scorers. But when I was a kid, my friends were just like hers are now. I survived them."

People love to run down teenagers. They pour it on, how terrible teens are. The truth is that 98 percent of teens do okay. Most of us did okay, the exemplary kids and the not-so-exemplary kids. These kids are facing all kinds of losses. We lost the same things. We got by. True, times were different twenty years ago, or ten, or thirty, but if we explore our memories of the past fully, we will see how, down at the bottom line, we triumphed over doom and did all right. So will the kids.

Lorraine illustrates one other point as well. Teenagers are remarkably forgiving of adults' blunders if the adults' hearts are in the right place.

Hope is a positive thing, and good memories foster hope best. Although bad memories are usually what come to mind most readily, kids hungrily seek good ones. We can help.

Building Good Memories

Why do I get up before the crack of dawn on Saturdays to take my daughters and their horses to gymkhanas and rides?

Why do I take my kids out to a ranch a state away, driving for many hours just to have a day or two of fun? Why do I tell them goofy stories? Supervise their choices of television and movie entertainment? Pay close attention to their daily environment?

Mary Alice and I are taking care to implant good memories. Teenagers are so vulnerable. So vulnerable! Even where there is no abuse or trauma, kids are still preciously sensitive. Their whole world rises and falls on the approval of that other person, and "that other person" can be any of a hundred people in their lives.

Memories are being forged every moment. Think of the opportunity for parents to make positive memories!

We hear all sorts of stories from our radio listeners; the exchanges between our listeners and us is always my favorite part of the show. Some stories are joyful and others are tragic, but they all touch deeply. One of my favorites is from a radio listener who told about a father and son situation. The father bought tickets for a Chicago Bulls game, but he didn't tell his son. After taking his son out to dinner, he asked, "Now what?"

Jokingly, his son suggested, "Let's stand outside the Bulls arena and buy someone's tickets for three hundred bucks."

His dad replied, "Or just use these," and he dropped them in his son's lap.

What a wonderful story! Do you see why that memory is so precious? It's not the tickets themselves, but the love behind them—the relationship.

In part four I want to devote several chapters just to building good memories. It is so important. Regardless of how you build good memories in your teenager, you will base them on a good, or improving, relationship.

Healing works for kids, especially older kids, just as it does for adults, in ways we have already examined. But there are wonderful, proactive ways in which you can help children like Chad Houser whose mind works in a unique way. We'll look at how to meet those special needs in chapter 12.

Meeting a Child's Special Memory Needs

He was a royal pain in grade school. His high school advisor quickly shunted him into special education classes and warned him to never go to college. Today, Rick Fowler, with a full complement of educational achievement behind him, is the author of a number of important books dealing with psychological issues. He serves as one of our best and brightest counselors at the Minirth Meier Clinic. Says Dr. Brian Newman, another of our counselors, "Rick overcame so much. He's a personal inspiration and model."

"I felt really guilty that I couldn't learn, that my memory was so bad," Rick claims. "The other kids did just fine, so obviously there was something wrong with me. Everyone told me I wasn't trying hard enough."

What was "wrong" with Rick Fowler was not wrong at all in the proper sense of the word. It was different. His problem is Attention Deficit Hyperactivity Disorder (ADHD), a difference affecting hundreds of thousands of children and adults.

Adjusting to the Brain's Needs

Elaine listened to Rick Fowler's story. "Yes. That's Chad's problem right there. We must have told him a thousand times he has to try harder. He has to pay attention better. But it's like water off a duck's back. He won't. Or he can't."

He couldn't. Chad's memory was just as capable of learning and functioning as anyone else's, but there were some crucial differences. One of the greatest of those differences was that Chad's memory could not absorb and retain information the way most schools present it and the way most people absorb it. In order to successfully insert certain kinds of information into his memory, Chad and his parents would have to use different means. In effect, they had to adjust learning techniques to Chad's particular situation.

The usual everyday schooling methods, by which most children build up an extensive trove of general somatic data with which to work in life, would do nothing for Chad as they did nothing for Rick.

"General somatic data. That's everyday information, right? Like Columbus discovered America and water freezes at 32 degrees." Now Ron Houser was getting very interested.

"Right."

"I have trouble with that kind of stuff. Not serious trouble, but trouble," Ron said.

I nodded, for the tale is a familiar one. Very frequently an adult whose child is diagnosed with Attention Deficit Hyperactivity Disorder learns, in adulthood, that the condition has been a problem throughout his or her own life. And in almost every instance, that adult has spent a lifetime thinking he or she was stupid or somehow at fault.

The way that an adult finds out, usually, is by noticing that he or she has a problem obtaining and retaining memorized data.

Rick likens it to coaching a basketball team with two guys six feet six inches as they compete against a team with two guys seven feet tall. Obviously, if the team's going to win, they have to keep those seven-footers away from the basket.

In our schools where the game of learning is played, the rules are skewed strongly toward the seven-footers. That is, the schools teach according to what might be called a left-brain system. You memorize facts and spit them out on cue. Learn in class, study, take the test, and pass.

Rick couldn't do that. Factual, sequential concepts are left-brain stuff, and he simply was not wired that way. Like other Attention Deficit Hyperactivity Disorder kids, Rick had to learn not by rote memorization but by hands-on drawing, touching, feeling, and experiencing. Right-brain stuff. And yet, learn he did, once he quit playing the usual school game and perfected the full court press of right-brain learning that enabled him to win.

People differ profoundly when it comes to learning and memorization. One of the differences is in the way the two halves of our brain differ and how much each of the two controls how we function in life.

One Difference: Left Versus Right

You've heard a lot of information, misinformation, and jokes about right brain versus left brain. In one episode of the old cartoon series *Bloom County*, Opus (an out-and-out right brainer if ever there was one) sat on a grassy hillside talking to the computer whiz character about right- and left-brain matters. As Opus babbled on wistfully, the computer whiz tilted, then fell over onto his left side, a cartoon indication that his left brain hemisphere was so much heavier. References like that crop up everywhere, for everyone knows about right brain versus left brain. The references and humor are firmly based in reality.

Identifying the Difference

Our brain is actually two separate brains, divided down the middle between the nose and the back of the head. The two halves communicate with each other by a tough, resilient connection at the base. The right side deals primarily with affective matters. These are feelings, creativity, the physical and manipulative, the artistic. The right side is not bound to one plus two equals three.

The left side deals primarily with logic, linear thought, organization, facts, the abstract. To the left brain, one plus two forever and always equals three.

Most people use both hemispheres more or less equally, although they probably will favor one over the other. This is one of the ways stereotypes arise. For example, stereotyping says that the artistic person will have trouble balancing the checkbook. People who are intensely creative are supposed to be poor business minds. People who quickly grasp such abstracts as numbers and formulae—the scientists and mathematicians—are expected to lack a strong interest in feelings.

Stereotypes aside, the norm of most people using both hemispheres proportionally is occasionally altered, sometimes even before birth. For example, during prenatal development boy babies experience a surge of testosterone that can prevent some of the nerve connections between hemispheres from forming. When the left brain takes over the majority of function, we call the child brilliant. When the right brain takes over, however, we call the result Attention Deficit Hyperactivity Disorder. A better term is Attention Deficit Hyperactivity *Difference*. That's not adequate, either, for *deficit* is so negative. Because of that simple, natural, prenatal testosterone effect, more boys are ADHD kids than are girls, although girls can be affected just as severely.

When the norm is altered, trouble can result. The trouble is generated not by the shortcomings of the people who differ from the norm but rather by the way outsiders measure them. Many psychological tests, most intelligence tests, and nearly all scholastic aptitude tests are geared to left-brain systems. They completely leave out the right-brain kids.

Right-brain kids have trouble with short-term memory. If

you give Rick a five-digit number, mention aloud some other numbers—a phone number, perhaps, or a social security number—and then ask Rick to repeat the five-digit number, he can't. Psychological tests based on the left brain would indicate that Rick and others like him have psychological problems, difficulties processing material. No, that's not true at all. That's just how those particular brains work.

So how does a right-brain person like Rick compensate in this left brain idolizing world? Rick learned to master this particular difference, but it certainly wasn't easy for him.

Adjusting for the Difference

"You don't outgrow it," says Rick. "You learn to cope with it. I write everything down. And I file things."

Because the right-brain person's internal, mental organization is not lockstep orderly, that person's external organization must be. Rick seems overly organized because all his organization is on the outside. "The object is not perfection but balance," he explains. "Super external organization brings balance because you are naturally so terribly disorganized internally. Don't try to be perfect. Just try to bring it to the middle."

Keep the facts and data you need immediately at hand according to some sort of system. Know where you can get the information you need if you cannot stash that information directly in your memory.

In other words, compensate.

Attention Deficit Hyperactivity Disorder affects both memory capacity (rather, the ability to both encode and retrieve memory) and style of retrieval. Stress tunes the mind out. So does factual overload. When faced with a large amount of new material to process, the ADHD person's mind will divert. ADHD kids are accused of daydreaming, of letting their minds wander. They actually have no control over that. Their minds simply go ahead and do it, as when Chad Houser abandoned the study of nouns and thought instead about painting his Housermobile.

Because stress causes the ADHD person's mind to jump the track, stress reduction is essential for learning and memorization in ADHD people. Little kids have trouble mastering stress reduction techniques. In fact, they can't do it on their own because not only do they not understand what stress is, they have no depth of experience for building some alternative way of doing things. They are strictly a product of their surroundings. If their stress level is to be reduced, parents and teachers must reduce it for them.

Adults can manage stress reduction better. They have better resources and deeper understanding. They can separate themselves from situations in ways that kids cannot.

Another way to prevent overload is to consolidate materials and place them in an arrangement you can picture. Says Rick, "I condense twenty pages of notes down to one sheet. Then I visualize on that sheet where the material is. Twenty sheets were overload. One I can deal with."

A friend of mine has studied Scripture for many years. She's a right-brain person, and you should see her Bible. It is not only a particular translation, it is a particular edition of that translation. She bought four identical copies of that edition at the same time and put three of them in a drawer. She also bought colored pencils and a red notebook. When she studies a passage she colors lines or paragraphs with a pencil according to an extensive color coding system she wrote down on the flyleaf. Brief notes and insights and cross-references she writes in the wide margins of that particular edition. More extensive notes and essays go into the notebook. The notebook page number then is penciled in red in the Bible's margin. When she filled the red notebook she bought a blue one and wrote in page numbers with a blue pencil. She's into her fifth notebook now. She couldn't find a notebook bound in yellow or green, so she covered the spine of a black one with yellow bookbinder's tape and another with green.

And those three other copies in her drawer? When she literally wore out her first copy, she painstakingly transferred her notes, colors and all, to a new copy. It was very important for her to have the chapters and verses identically arranged in both copies, and that you get only with multiple copies of the same edition. "You see, " she explained, "I cannot remember chapter-and-verse numbers to save me. But I can remember where I saw it spatially on the page. For instance, it was in the lower left column of the left page, say. So I might thumb through twenty pages of a book, watching the lower left corner, and there it will be eventually. My spacial orientation is just fine. My numbers are atrocious."

Like Rick, then, she compensates. She leaves no insights or notes to memory. When many people think, "Oh, I'll remember that," it turns out that they do, perhaps for years afterward. She cannot. She knows that she can easily remember the physical location of a passage because that's the way her brain works. So she uses the way her brain remembers in order to find what she needs rather than punish herself with the futile, frustrating, impossible task of trying to memorize the chapter and verse numbers.

Can she find the passage she wants when she wants it? As fast as anyone else!

This difference about brains, a major one, raises issues that affect parent-child relationships. We deal with a lot of ADHD parents as well as kids. Although ADHD people are never too old to improve by learning better compensation techniques, the sooner the difference is diagnosed, the sooner the child can get help. Also, a parent without a strong right-brain orientation too often cannot understand the child who has one.

"My kid is lazy. He just doesn't apply himself."

"My kid would rather run around and daydream than work."

"My kid is stupid."

It's so sad! Think what those messages do to a child when he or she hears them from infancy on. They become self-fulfilling. Devastating. That child is not lazy or stupid, but until parent and child learn how to develop the memory *as it is*, the frictions and frustrations will remain.

All this sounds as though ADHD people are at best weird and at worst hopelessly handicapped. Not at all. They do a lot of things better than average people can.

The Advantages of ADHD

The Housermobile is a brilliant testimony to Chad's creativity. Creativity and resourcefulness come through very strongly in ADHD and right-brain people because they are able to think globally.

The global thinker, as opposed to the linear thinker, reaches out in all directions to tap memories, so to speak. Linear thinking proceeds in a straight line. One plus one is two. To achieve goal D we must move from A through B through C. The global thinker might get from A to D by skipping up and over to S through Q and down to E then back to D.

Small children start out thinking globally. This is what makes them so good at short-term memory games like Concentration. It's really hard to beat a four year old at Concentration. Left-brain oriented people build and improve their linear thinking as they get older. Right-brain people do so to a lesser degree. It is all a matter of how the person accesses memory.

Although he had trouble with the rote memorization of facts and he tuned out when overloaded, Chad did a fine job of blotting up his surroundings. In fact, he developed his episodic memory better than do many people. By the age of ten, Chad, like most ADHD people, already enjoyed a broad range of choices to draw from with his global thinking, a wide variety of episodic information. This works; that does not. This operates in this way; that operates in a different way.

"I can see that," Elaine said. "But how can Chad succeed in school when the usual teaching methods don't work for him? How can I help him?"

Learning in New Ways

There are a number of things Ron and Elaine did to encourage Chad's success.

Provide access to good reference material

Because ADHD people cannot accumulate general somatic data well, they need the resources in which to find it. A good dictionary and a good encyclopedia should be in every home but especially in the homes of ADHD people. Ron and Elaine provided Chad with extra incentive to develop good library skills by going with him to the library. Nothing instills good library skills in kids like frequent library visits with their parents.

Remind him of helpful pointers

When children in school fail to thrive with normal teaching methods, they get discouraged. Using Rick Fowler's tips for compensating can help them succeed, but they don't always think of them on their own.

Encourage the kind of memory work she does best—episodic and procedural

This does two things: it broadens further the person's range of memories upon which to draw when needed, and by stimulating the memory it promotes the ability to memorize.

Promote hands-on learning

Ron and Elaine ended up hiring a tutor for this. Although ADHD persons have trouble with rote memorization, they can learn quickly and well through physical manipulation and other mechanical means. Using an abacus comes naturally to them. It's visual and manual.

"The science center!" Ron laughed. "We took the kids to the science center where they have all these hands-on experiments and devices. I had more fun than the kids. No, that's not true. Chad was in seventh heaven."

Seek out discovery centers, nature centers, and other education adjuncts of museums and parks. The ADHD person needs to handle the lesson, watch it, physically make contact.

Encourage doing; emphasize the concrete over the abstract

Doing is what ADHD people are best at. The more they do, the better they become at doing, at thinking, and at remembering.

"Chad had to learn about nouns recently," Elaine said. "That's very abstract for a ten year old. How can I help him make it concrete or manipulative?"

One possibility an educator suggested was to direct him to make flashcards of words that he would later assemble as sentences. Nothing fancy. Simple strips of paper, either hand-printed or run through a computer and printer, plus blank strips for additional words as needed.

Let him physically assemble sentences, laying the strips out on a flat surface. Using *red* as an adjective, make a sentence. Use *red* as a noun and make a sentence. In the first it describes something, in the second it is the name of a color. The lesson comes to his memory through his hands and eyes.

As Chad got into the swing of it, he might concoct deliberate nonsense, and for him that would be instructive. He would be seeing how the language works by exploring how it does not work. The ADHD kid is good at that. Global thinking, remember? Coming at it backward and sideways. He may not be able to memorize rote rules, but he can see how things work.

Elaine could also help Chad and her daughter, Stephanie, to grow in healthy ways. That involves creating happy memories to take the place of sad ones, building positive memories to replace negative messages.

The best part of all, it's fun!

WHEN MEMORIES BUILD THE FUTURE

13

Building Good Family Memories

In a delightful one-panel cartoon by *Family Circus* artist Bil Keane, the family is returning from vacation, cruising down the road in their loaded station wagon. Parents and kids are all reviewing their happy memories, expressed in thought balloons. In the parents' balloons are waterfalls, mountains, and other scenic wonders. In the kids' are fast food joints, carnivals, zoos, a miniature golf course . . .

It's, oh, so true.

How-To

Kids need a trove of good memories, but their parents need them just as much. They may not be the same memories—not too many adults wax ecstatic over a fast food emporium—but good memories are absolutely necessary to every human being for building a healthy life. We might divide building good memories into considerations of *persons*, *places*, and *things*, plus a fourth designation, *activities*. Before we get rolling, let me suggest some general operating procedures.

Plan

Rarely does a good memory just happen. Oh, sure, it's possible, but life is too short to wait around for it. Plan in three ways:

Ask, "Is what we are doing/saying/being right now going to provide a positive memory?" Minimize activities, conversations, and situations where you would have to waffle with the answer. "Well, uh, maybe not, but, uh . . ." Maximize all those things that allow an answer of a hearty "Yes!"

Literally plan events. They don't have to be elaborate, but they do have to be set up. If you're going to the zoo, decide where you'll have lunch. Picnic? Zebraburger? Restaurant? You need to obtain tickets in advance. You may need to gather materials for projects. (You can minimize this by having a box of stuff on hand; we'll discuss that.)

Watch for the serendipitous occasion and plan something around it. Is the circus coming to town? How about a traveling dinosaur exhibit coming through or a temporary art exhibit? With as little as a few hours notice, you may be able to arrange something great.

Keep It Simple

Difficulties and unforeseen problems multiply exponentially as plans become elaborate. Besides, if you're making a good memory with kids involved, they do better by far with simple stuff than with complex activities.

If you are a single parent with limited contact with your kids, this keep-it-simple principle is especially important. Time is gold, and you want to spend it as wisely as possible. This does not mean scheduling every moment. It means relaxing and spending it with the kids, not maintaining some elaborate plan. The very best activities are the casual visits, the easy-going stuff, and the mere goofing off.

Don't Expect Perfection

Things are going to go wrong. Sometimes the hits, runs, and errors turn out to be more fun than the original plan. Flexibility will help a lot when weather aces you out, you miss a train, or one of the kids gets sick.

"That's good," Ron said, as he told me about an outing at a beach on Grapevine Lake. "We accidentally locked the car keys in the trunk; a rainstorm arrived at the beach the same time we did; Steph stepped on some kind of little beetle that scared the willies out of her; Elaine got sunburned; and I nearly drowned when I waded out and stepped in a hole. What a day. The kids are still laughing."

The kids are still laughing. What a paean to a happy day!

"Incidentally," I asked, "how did you get the keys out of the trunk?"

"Good old Chad to the rescue. He used his new pocket knife as a screwdriver to get a taillight off, reached in the little hole with his skinny arm, groped around, and found them."

Score one for Chad!

Your good memories are never going to turn out perfect 100 percent of the time, so it pays to allow for that in advance. It will help you greatly to ease over the speed bumps in your freeway of life.

Remember the Value of Goof-Off Time

Children in particular need unstructured time to simply vegetate.

"Chad doesn't. He goofs off too much," Elaine said, looking sternly at her son.

"We'll discuss that," I promised. "But, yes. He needs it too."

Kids are not vegetating, actually, as they goof off. Their little minds are going a mile a minute below conscious level, processing what they have been observing lately. Adults also need unstructured time. These goof-off hours can provide memories as rich and beautiful as any scheduled event. They are never wasted time! Make sure they occur in abundance in your family's world.

Family History Is Important!

Whatever the activity or event, keep the family's history in mind. Kids need a strong connection with their past if they are going to feel that they belong. It promotes a sense of security to know that there is a broad extended family out there, in the present and in the past, and you're a part of it. Plan and execute good-memory events with the family's history in mind whenever possible, remembering all the while that you are creating the history your children will remember in their later years. You, your kids, and your parents all are part of a continuum. It's not stopping here.

"No." A woman we'll call Sandra was not about to get into her family history. "My father is an alcoholic, my mom has mental problems, my grandfather served time at San Quentin, and both my uncles are jerks like you wouldn't believe. The less my kids know about the family's history, the better off they are."

I didn't say bright, cheery, something-to-be-proud-of history. I said family history. Certainly Sandra should be judicious about what she will tell her small children. But by the time they reach adulthood, your children should know the good, the bad, and the ugly about their family.

You never know. For instance, just prior to 1800, England established several penal colonies in Australia. Convicts transported there worked out terms of seven years or more. Many stayed in Australia when their terms were completed and two populations resulted: the people who were once prisoners and the people who arrived free. Not more than a generation ago in Australia it was still a matter of shame if your ancestors came over as prisoners. Today, Aussies look back with pride to their convict ancestors, people strong enough to turn desperate adversity into a rewarding life. Give your children the drum, as the Aussies say. That is, tell them the truth and all the truth.

You might want to establish a family archive. A file carton or two will suffice. In them stash letters, photos, yearbooks, articles—whatever touches on family history.

Sandra's attitude toward her family aside, how might she and you build good memories? You start with people.

People

Let's subdivide *people*, a pretty inclusive category, into *family*, *others* (neighbors, friends, and total strangers), and *self*. Each group provides plenty of fodder for making good memories.

Family

Your family, whether it is made up of a single person— you—or a passel of folks, will benefit if you build ritual right into the family structure. Ritual and tradition are the building blocks of stability. If you have children at home, ritual becomes particularly valuable. Kids groove on familiar ritual. It becomes their security. The world may bluster and threaten, but at home we wash our hands before coming to the table. We go to bed at such-and-so time. We maintain a stately order against the chaos of the outside. Ritual is so comforting.

Usually, the mother sets the tone of the household, and the father establishes the environment for memories. This isn't sexual stereotyping, it's just the way things normally are.

Randy Carlson recalls, "In Salem, Virginia, way back when, I'd go down to the church with my father who was the minister of education, early Sunday before things got started. I'd help him run the old ditto machine, get the construction paper ready, a lot of little jobs. We'd stop every moment or two and get doughnuts and coffee. I remember an immense emotional pride in the man, and I was doing something for which I was proud of myself."

People. Memories.

Make one meal a day a sit-down family affair

Break out the candles, centerpiece, napkins, tablecloth, or matching placemats, the whole nine yards. Candlelight has the beneficial effect of quieting kids and grown-ups alike. It provides a peaceful, relaxed atmosphere, exactly what you need for pleasant memories. This of course should be a time of conversation and sharing (*not* preaching by Dad, whining by kids, complaining by Mom, begging by the dog).

Are you putting on airs? Hardly! This goes beyond ritual and routine. You have just provided a forum, a thing family members may not have out in the world. It contributes to pleasant memories and an abiding sense of security that, like the sun coming up and going down, the family will do certain things regularly. Adults thrive on it just as much as do kids. There is a tranquility to following a certain pattern daily, so long as you don't slip into slavery to it. It's also nice to break the pattern now and then.

May, a widow, says, "We used to do that every single night, my husband and I. After he passed away, I couldn't find the energy to keep it up. But I missed it. I was so used to it, you know? So I compromise now. I sit myself down at a table for a full meal once or twice a week. Candles, napkins, the whole thing, like we used to do. Ritual is what it is, and comforting. And I prepare a fairly large meal, guaranteeing lots of leftovers. I eat the next evenings' meals at the kitchen counter, usually with a pencil and crossword puzzle book, until the leftovers run out. Then I prepare myself a 'real' meal again."

May's attention to ritual and tradition gives her an added

bonus, something very many older people fail to provide themselves—a good, well-rounded diet.

Plan time together

Saturday morning the girls and I get up at 4:30, load the horses, stop at a favorite breakfast spot for biscuits and gravy, and from there go riding, attend a gymkhana, enter a horse show. These Saturdays don't just happen, you know. And ah, the memories!

"Oh, yeah? Planning. Right. What about the unplanned emergencies and vehicle breakdowns and the times things went wrong?"

They are as much a part of the memories as the blue ribbons and silly fun. We got through the setbacks and past them and over them. They have become life lessons as valuable as any other. Practical lessons as well as lessons in theory. Believe me, my girls know how to change a tire.

Long-distance contact works

Try sending videotapes or cassette recordings to family members and close friends. Get a round-robin letter going through the far-flung family. Buy a simple disposable camera, take some pictures, and send the whole camera.

Says a friend from Pennsylvania, "Cassette tape? It almost didn't work. My family are all Dutchmen from the Lancaster area, speaking with a strong regional accent. They cut one tape, heard themselves, and got all embarrassed. Fortunately, they sent it anyway. We still have it, a link between them and our own grandkids." Good fruit from a project that looked like it might have gone sour!

Write to the family

"When my kids found out about Granpop doing time at Q, they were thrilled." Sandra gulped in consternation at the memory. "They kept pestering me. Finally, against my better judgment, I let them write to him. They took days putting together that first letter. I just wish they'd spend that much time and effort on their homework! He was in an old folks' home near Castroville by that time. We had to really fish around to find the address; called the chamber of commerce and everything."

Sandra's eyes grew misty. "Granpop sent the most wonderful letter back. He talked about what he had done wrong and how he wished he could do it all right this time. Yes, he preached to them! Obey the law and keep their noses clean was the way he said it. And I could talk till I'm blue in the face without reaching those kids the way his letter did.

"You know, that old man was so lonely, and wishing he knew what became of me and my brothers, and whether we had any kids. The children's letter was a godsend to him.

"Right away the kids started up a correspondence, sent pictures and everything. He died a couple years later during the night of a massive stroke. His latest letter to the kids was on his bedside table half finished when they found him."

More good fruit. This does not mean that every project you devise to establish and maintain contact with your extended family is going to work. Some won't. Several people I know tried to get contact going and the other family members dropped the ball.

Others

Neighbors, the elderly, other family members—what a kaleidoscope of people! There are memories here for everyone. Two classes of people exist, those who serve and those who are served. And the classes intermingle. She who serves today might appreciate being served tomorrow. Kids enjoy serving others. Encourage them in it. Kids especially enjoy being the center of attention themselves. Serve them on occasion.

When I was growing up, I was surrounded by godly elderly people. They treated me like a favorite grandson, and didn't I eat that up! They were wonderful people. Today I just like elderly people instantly. You see, my attitude today is a direct result of the good memories I had growing up. So keep in mind that people are shaping your future responses to people.

To me elderly people seem especially compassionate. How do you teach children compassion? By taking them along as you reach out. How about:

- Mowing an elderly neighbor's lawn, gardening, or raking leaves
- Walking the dog next door; making a pet toy for the cat
- Driving persons places or handling groceries
- Working at an animal control shelter (that's a dog pound), mission facility (adults and older kids only—don't send really small kids in there), or charitable institution
- Volunteer at the park, zoo, botanical garden, church, historical facility, library, or hospital

If possible, choose adult jobs kids can handle or help with. This is serious stuff, this practical aid to others, and it is immensely rewarding. It's not kid stuff.

If you have no kids around, don't let that slow you down. You will find a treasure of good memories in helping others.

Self

You are as much a person as anyone else is, and you deserve as much of your own attention as does anyone else. To promote good memories and especially to counteract bad ones, avoid people who tear others down. Gravitate as much as possible to people who build others up. You also must be a builder. Listen to your own self-talk and make certain it is comprised of things you ought to be hearing. You need people who are pleasant without being cloying, honest without being harsh.

Especially, let Christ build you up through reading His Word. You are essentially reprogramming yourself to take in new messages and new memories which will eventually shove bad ones to the back of your mind. His Word is full of builder-uppers.

Places can also yield fond memories for you and the other people in your life.

Places

For nearly forty years, Dan S. worked for the Jersey Central Railroad. His office was on the Jersey shore. The Statue of Liberty was outside his window with her back toward him. In those forty years he never once visited the Statue of Liberty.

In Vancouver, Washington, between a city park and the Columbia River bank, sits Fort Vancouver National Historical Monument. Everyone in the nation recognizes the monument's national importance except, by and large, the people of Vancouver.

What are you overlooking in your immediate area? There are almost certainly nearby places of prominent interest.

Visit the Local Sights

Few places in the world lack important features in their immediate vicinity. I can think of half a dozen big attractions and sites of interest in the Dallas area where I live and work, and another half dozen on the way to our place in Arkansas. Any one of them would provide a relaxed, pleasant day's excursion.

Allow Ample Time

Take the time to visit and explore. Interesting things turn

up. I'm thinking now of the friend of a friend who lived near Lone Pine, California. One afternoon he was driving the long, lonely road south down the Panamint Valley when a small glider coasted silently over his head and landed southbound on the road before him. The friend helped the pilot pull the glider off the highway. He took the time to drive the glider pilot the forty miles back to the north end of the valley to rejoin his companions.

To quote the friend: "All of a sudden I find myself up in this glider two thousand feet above the valley. And I'm thinking to myself, 'Great Caesar's toga! What am I doing up here?' "

What he was doing was having a ball. He took time out to help a stranger in a strange situation, was rewarded with a splendid glider tour, and added a great memory not only to his own trove but to those of the friends to whom he told the story.

Plan Vacations with Memories in Mind

A few years ago one of my children complained, "We never go on a vacation." That floored me. I travel a lot, to conferences and speaking engagements, and I always take at least some of the family along. Sometimes we all go. Sometimes it's just one of the girls. What did she mean, we never took a vacation?

"That's just it, Dad. It's never a vacation. It's a business trip with some other stuff thrown in. I mean, you know, a real *vacation*."

And you know what? She was right. I still take one or more kids along on business trips. But we also take real vacations.

While you're planning:

- Turn the kids loose with the maps and tour books and see what they come up with.
- Play games along the way. "Can you find . . . a red

barn? A white horse?" Adults can give this a grown-up twist that makes games fun for anyone.

- Center a vacation around a theme or purpose. I have friends, avid bird-watchers, who go to places where they are likely to find unusual birds. Another friend seeks out railroads. He's done the Durango-Silverton run in Colorado several times. He traveled to Pennsylvania just to visit the Strasburg Railroad Museum. What are your interests?

- Spend vacation time with friends if possible. If you have kids, try to take a vacation with another couple with kids. If you're older go on tour with friends. Good friends multiply good memories.

Don't Be Afraid to Repeat Tried and True Situations

At least once a year I take each of the girls out to our ranch in Arkansas for a weekend. Just the two of us. We talk, sing, ride, fish, explore. We enjoy each other's company. We relax and unwind. Yes, even the kids need relief from tight schedules and heavy responsibilities. Our family goes to the same place over and over because there we find peace. Respite is a happy memory in itself.

I don't just take those special trips for the kids' sakes. I love them too. For example, when Carrie and I went camping, we rode the horses back in the mountains and went canoeing. It's a beautiful memory for me because I've never forgotten the camping I did with my dad. The past feelings and present episodes mix into a soft tapestry of memories.

What memories do you want to perpetuate?

Things

You know those little roses some people make by winding narrow satin ribbon? A woman named Nancy found herself in charge of a large banquet. Fifteen hundred people were expected. She chose a remembrance (a goldtone business card case with the event's name engraved) and ordered fifteen hundred of them. She decided that as a favor for each attendee, the card case, the banquet program, and some handouts were to be wrapped together in a pink ribbon and topped with little roses. She needed, in all, 4,500 roses. So, she purchased half a dozen of the spindles with which you make ribbon roses. Every time friends would drop by she would hand them a spindle and show them how to do it. As friends and neighbors and total strangers sat in her dining room chatting, they made ribbon roses. She made ribbon roses on the bus going to work. She made ribbon roses on her lunch hour. In less than three months she had all the roses she needed. The elegant ribbon-wrapped banquet favors, need I say, were beautiful.

The ribbon roses project served a far more extensive purpose than banquet favors. The craft, productive and easy to catch onto, provided a conversation magnet.

Conversation Magnets

Call a conversation magnet an alternative focus. People sit around and talk, yes. But conversation proceeds far more easily if they have some alternative focus, such as busy work for their hands. This is one of the reasons the first thing you say when someone comes to visit is, "What can I get for you?" Conversation goes better with coffee or iced tea to sip. Those ribbon roses provided a very satisfying alternative focus, as well as being fun to wind. Guests were making a positive contribution. You could see the results. Talk flowed freely. Nancy commented on how much pleasure she took from friends' visits during the project.

If you have the space, spread a 500- or 1,000-piece jigsaw puzzle out on a coffee table. When people drop by, work on the puzzle as you chat. Jigsaw puzzles make wonderful magnets and provide lovely memories.

"Hmph," mumbled a grizzled old farmer. "If that's the way it works, I'll hand folks an axe. I got four cords of winter stovewood to split."

Sorry. Not everything works as a conversation magnet.

Holidays

Holidays. What fond memories!

"Hardly!" Sandra said. "Believe me, in the home of an alcoholic, holidays are the worst times of the year. That's when fights and booze and ugliness are at their most terrible. I have no happy memories of my childhood holidays. None."

What about a person like Sandra who owns no happy holiday memories? Sandra had worked past her problems herself. But she still couldn't invite her parents for the holidays. They caused too many difficulties and generated too much friction. After a couple disastrous years, her husband refused to take the kids to her parents' house as well, and he was not being unreasonable. Sandra didn't want her brothers coming around. They were disruptive and surly. On her husband's side of the family, only his mother still lived, and she was in Mexico. Yet, Sandra wanted her kids to have happy holiday memories and traditions to observe. She yearned for the richness in their lives that only tradition provides. How could she work around that and build good memories to supplant the bad?

"I called a family meeting," Sandra said. "That's what I always do when there's a problem. Let everyone solve it."

She explained to her husband and children what I described above. She asked their opinion. What did they want? How might they go about getting it?

The kids came up with the solution to their dearth of pleasant traditions. Her eldest son, then seven, phrased it poorly, but he had a good idea. "Steal other people's."

"Better," Sandra cajoled, "let's borrow."

At school, at the library, from the neighbors, Sandra's

husband and kids asked about traditions and holiday activities. They brought their findings to another meeting around the dining table, and from the complete list they chose some traditions to try as their own.

Christmas came and passed.

Dreamy-eyed that Christmas night, her little son purred, "This was so happy! This was the best Christmas ever. Nobody could have a Christmas like this one!"

Sandra couldn't reply because she was too choked up. This was the first time in her life that between Christmas Eve and Christmas night no one had to call the police.

If you don't have traditions, borrow them

If you have no holiday traditions handed down from the past or if the traditions you have simply don't work well, by all means do as Sandra's family did. Borrow. Over the years they abandoned a few ideas and added others. So, when you cast about seeking new ideas to try, keep in mind that you will likely be "stuck" with them, and happily so. Therefore, choose sparingly. Don't overload.

If you have too many traditions, abandon some

Too many traditions? How can that be?

"I know what you're talking about. I used to be in that pit," Elaine Houser said. "We were so buried in traditions and busy-ness that holidays weren't fun anymore. We were running around too much, trying to do too much. I finally had to call a halt. We still did the advent wreath, for example, and the tree, but I gave up the baking. All of it. Cold turkey. It was the nicest Christmas in a decade. And nobody missed it. We slimmed the schedule down even more the next year. Less is more."

Less is more. If you are looking for good memories, rushing around won't provide them. Go for quality, not quantity.

Quality is greatly enhanced if you draw others into your plans or arrange for others to benefit.

Include others

Here's a tradition for you. At the house of a man I'll call Bill, he and his wife bake dozens of sugar cookies every year. Then they sit down and, with food coloring and confectioners' sugar, they paint the cookies. The kids used to join in but the kids are grown now. Still, Bill and Marge carry on. Every house on their block receives a paper plate of cookies. On that plate are a few plain cookies, some fancy painted ones, and a cookie with his or her name painted on it for each person in the house. The neighborhood dogs each get a bone-shaped one. Bill and Marge deliver the cookies on Christmas Eve, and invoke God's blessing specifically on each neighbor and house as they go.

Including others enriches memories as nothing else can.

Note that Bill and Marge did not establish their cookie tradition for the purpose of giving their kids a warm memory. They did it as a vehicle for asking God's blessing on their friends. The kids absorbed it, of course, but it was not an activity specifically for them.

Books

Books are perhaps the richest source of memories you will find. How many of us remember treasured old books, some of them so fragile and yellowed they are no longer readable?

"Some of the books on my shelf," says a friend, Evelyn Wye, "are the ones we kids read when we were tiny. Some are brand new. There are wonderful new books on the market these days and a lot of classics still available. I get kids' books sometimes just for myself—and for when the grandkids come over, of course."

Reading is the finest memory you can give kids, and children hardly ever grow up as readers unless reading is promoted in the home during their childhood. Here is where making good memories pays dividends in other ways as well.

Evelyn Wye keeps books always at hand. But that's not all she keeps.

Activities

She calls it her Granny Bag. It's a tote bag made out of plastic canvas, decorated with a frog on one side. In it Evelyn Wye keeps crayon, paper, dominoes, some simple games, cut-and-paste paper airplanes, books, scissors, and paste. These are *Granny's* toys. Fortunately, for her three small grandchildren, she has learned to share nicely. When the kids come over the Granny Bag comes out, and they enjoy endless delights for days at a time. Why the frog? No particular reason. Evelyn adopted the frog as a sort of symbol. Now whenever the kids see pictures of frogs, they think of Granny.

Eveyln doesn't mind a bit. She says, "I came out ahead. It could have been a pig."

Keep Supplies on Hand

Evelyn makes sure she has plenty of supplies for art and craft projects, not just for her grandchildren, but for herself as well. She learned origami last year, for instance, and now she keeps a deck of interesting rice papers. If you have kids or entertain kids, you will want a stash of plain paper, markers or crayons, scissors, paste, and tape. That's all you need.

What is your pleasure? Needlework? Carving? Woodworking? Make sure your hobby is well supplied in an accessible place. Nothing kills a hobby quicker than the lack of the one thing you need for a project or the space to comfortably pursue it.

In the small towns near where I grew up and on the farms, women didn't have easy access to the eye-popping variety of sewing notions and craft supplies women today can find. Every woman who pursued needlework, and there were many, kept a good supply of crochet cotton, quilt scraps, pins and needles, yarn and embroidery floss. You need size ten shaded yellow for a doily? Go next door and borrow it from Maude. Maude will be at your door next week because she ran out of brown six-strand floss.

These days with stores so close, most people don't keep a stock of supplies at hand, and as a result they are often thwarted when they went to build or make or do something as recreation. If you enjoy a hobby or avocation, keep supplied. Beautiful memories come from the pursuit of favorite hobbies.

Nearly fifty years ago, Allie, who was then in her thirties, spent many hours completing a gorgeous Christmas tablecloth with embroidered holly leaves and berries. Allie was a smoker, as were many people then. Her cigarette rolled off the ashtray and burned a hole in the middle of that beautiful tablecloth. She was distraught to say the least. Then she got out her needle and floss and carefully embroidered a holly berry to cover and mend the hole. She embroidered other berries to balance it, so it wouldn't stick out there all alone. This last year Allie's daughter copied the pattern and made a tablecloth almost exactly like her mother's. As a finishing touch she embroidered the extra berries in the middle, a tribute to her mother's triumph over adversity, loss, and sorrow.

So many memories attend that old tablecloth and the new one as well. I believe Allie's daughter was wise to honor the memory, even if it wasn't what some would call an altogether cheerful recollection. It speaks volumes about Allie's indomitable spirit, her skill, and her courage.

Cooking

You can eat your mistakes or feed them to the birds. Here is a great memory maker that anyone can enjoy alone or with others.

One of my friend Alyce's favorite photos was taken by her husband at his mother's house. His mother is an enthusiastic cook. In the foreground of the photo she is stirring a pan on the stove as Alyce's teenage daughter sits on a stool at the far end of the counter, intently writing down Grandma's recipe.

Cooking brings together tradition, fun, love, and practicality. It ties together the generations. No one tires of good food. Cooking can be done just about anywhere, even over a campfire. How many hundreds of S'Mores have my family and I devoured over a crackling campfire? Now I admit S'Mores aren't exactly gourmet cooking—a marshmallow and a piece of chocolate bar between graham crackers—but we're talking memories here, not gustatory greatness. On second thought, S'Mores indeed taste pretty great.

Use cooking as an alternative focus during family visits or as the center of holiday activities. Kids love it. So do adults.

And everyone loves games.

Games

"We had to give up croquet in our side yard," Sandra complained. "Every time we'd go out to play, our elderly neighbor, Mr. Sanborn, would come roaring out to join us. Talk about a cutthroat, play-to-kill attitude! And he cheated. We finally just gave up."

Sandra's croquet difficulties notwithstanding, she and her family quickly latched onto games as a great way to store up fond memories. Her kids relish the fast card games, like Uno. She and her husband have picked up Scrabble lately. They play Pictionary or one of the other games for several players whenever three or four couples get together.

Says Sandra, "This is all so new to me. When I was growing up we played solitaire behind a closed door if we played anything. If Dad thought we were goofing off, he'd fly into a rage. And when you have an alcoholic in your home, you never

ever invite friends over. It's too easy to be embarrassed or shamed. Games are great! I'm catching up on my childhood."

Talk about good memories to replace bad!

Most people enjoy fond memories of games in days past.

"I remember the all-night Monopoly games when I was fifteen or so," said Bill. "We'd loan each other thousands just to keep the game going."

"Parcheesi. When's the last time you played Parcheesi? We used to love it." Now Evelyn is teaching her grandkids Parcheesi, using the same old game board and wooden men of her own childhood.

"Rook. The kids at our end of the block could play Rook for four hours straight."

"Ever try to play Concentration with a three year old? Don't. Trust me on this. The kid will beat you every time."

The memories you make now will be the fond memories you and your kids will look back on in the future, just like the folks quoted above.

The Housers' kids built their own miniature golf course, following a suggestion in Gloria Gaither and Shirley Dobson's excellent book *Let's Make a Memory*. First they got Elaine and Ron to take them to play every mini-golf course within fifty miles. "Doing research," they explained. Then they made their own, quite an elaborate one, in fact, with moving ramps, a castle (out of 2-liter pop bottles and a plastic bucket) and a plastic inflatable *Tyrannosaurus rex*. I have no idea what part the dinosaur played.

One weekend the kids advertised a "play golf for the food bank" day. It was their own idea. They charged a donation of fifty cents and a can of food per person per round and invited the neighbors out to play their homemade course. They didn't do badly—$135 for the food bank and eight cartons of canned goods. (No, they didn't get 270 people through the course;

some folks went around three or four times, and others gave more than fifty cents).

Chad and Stephanie both received wonderful strokes of reassurance with that project. Chad had a major hand in the execution, and Stephanie handled the business details.

Afterward, Elaine sat down nose to nose with Steph and said, "Your father and I are immensely proud of you and your brother, not just because you achieved but because you both are such kind and giving people. You are beautiful!" She smiled. "And you're beautiful on the outside too."

Songs

My family and I often sing the old hymns together because songs elicit memories. Musical tunes are a tremendous trigger for calling up the past. Use music to create good memories.

Brian Newman recalls an old gentleman, an entertainer. "He sang a program of old hymns, and beautifully," Brian recalls. "Toward the end of his performance, he said, 'This one is going to bring back some memories for everyone here.' Then he sang 'In the Garden.' *Everybody* has memories associated with that old hymn. Everybody." Brian grins. "Hey. It worked for me. I remembered a man out of my past who sang that song well. It was a good memory."

Scripture

When is the last time you and your spouse shared favorite Bible verses? Something like that can be an excellent source of warmth and togetherness for the whole family.

Other Activities

Every person is different, even people who grew up under identical circumstances. You are different. You are special. Think about the memories you cherish and the memories you need. Use these suggestions not as blueprints but as jumping-off points as you build your own trove of precious memories.

For some people learning is an end in itself. They enjoy the process and the product—that is, increased memory. For me, the development of memory has a goal apart from itself. That is to learn better the mind and nature of God.

How do you fill your memory with things of God? Let's look at a few ways.

14

Blessed Memories

He paraphrases!" Elaine Houser said, absolutely glowing. "Ron and I tended to ride Chad pretty hard about not memorizing Scripture. After learning about his special memory needs, we got off that and asked him to learn what verses said. Not rote memorization. Just learning what the words conveyed. It's not as good as word-for-word by heart in some ways; we know that. But now Chad knows what it says and where it is in the Bible. He can find it, and that's so much better than before when he couldn't get anywhere. It's wonderful!"

Chad sat there beaming, just as proud. Maybe prouder. This was a heady new victory for him.

I asked him, "So did you learn John 3:16?"

He looked blank.

"For God so loved . . ."

A grin burst through the blank look like sunrise. "God loved the world so much that He let His Son die instead of us! Here. I'll show you." Chad popped his kids' easy-to-read large print Bible open—New King James, I noticed—and dug out John. "It's the front of the New Testament, sort of," he informed me. "And that verse is near the front end of John. In red." Within a minute or two he found it, and proudly, victoriously, he pointed it out.

Elaine had tears in her eyes.

Blessing Yourself with Memories

The person who isn't seriously into the Bible is likely to ask, "Why the big deal?" The person who depends upon daily infusions of Scripture knows the answer. Words in a book don't influence you much. Words in your heart and daily life guide you in both mundane and profound ways.

Use Your Memory for Practical Living

Solomon said in 1 Kings 3:9: "Give to Your servant an understanding heart [for I am inadequate as I am]."

Wisdom. The book of Proverbs extols wisdom. Is it any wonder that Psalms and Proverbs are often the first books to be memorized by people who desire to put the Scriptures to memory?

Verses fade if you don't use them. Way back in college I determined to memorize God's Word. (Randy Carlson, whose teachers wrote him off as a no-learner, has committed entire books of Scripture to memory.) And I have. But I need review every now and then. So I always have a couple memory verse cards in my suit coat pocket. I flip through them on a daily basis, reviewing, learning new ones. The cards are memory joggers, a solid peg to hang memories upon.

This is not to say there is no place for writing. I always recommend that the faithful start a prayer book. Write down the requests you make and have the adjacent column available to record the date the prayer was answered.

And to people who do not always "feel" saved, I suggest, "Make a fresh commitment right now and write the date in a

Bible. There it is, then, in black and white. Sometimes only black and white reassures completely."

Use the Word for Refreshment

We see a lot of pastors at the clinic. When Paul Meier and I were first starting the clinic, we wanted to bring a Christian perspective to our profession. Our first clients were nearly all ministering Christians, and they were hurting as much as anyone else hurts. Many of them suffered nothing more than spiritual and sometimes physical neglect. The press of duties and tasks robbed them of the time to nourish themselves. This is just as true of very many of the Christians who never see the inside of a clinic.

Therefore, we in the clinic strongly recommend to all servants—pastors especially—to spend time in God's Word just for the pleasure of it. Nothing to do with sermons. Not study. Not preparation for anything. Only for refreshment. Personal nourishment of the soul. It is necessary, but so few do it.

In the book of Joshua, Joshua had just been through a lot with God at his side. He was able to declare boldly, "As for me and my house, we will serve the Lord" (24:15). Wonderful! Then the next generation did it kind of by rote. It was expected. By the third generation, they didn't really know God anymore, and they were skidding down the pole toward serious trouble. The experience of God has to be fresh and immediate to every generation, not something learned. The person who has been refreshed in the Lord can say, "This is what God is to me now. He is here!"

Use God's Word to Keep a Proper Perspective on Old Memories

In this book I have cited a number of people who were victimized cruelly by others, their memories forever scarred as a result. The common comment they make is, "I understand the theory, but the practice is so hard."

I am delighted to be able to remind them of Romans 8:28, one of the most glorious, triumphant verses in all of Scripture. "And we know that all things work together for good to those who love God, to those who are called according to His purpose."

As the light comes on I hear them respond, "I see. Not all things are good. What happened to me was not good. But God will use those things anyway."

Bingo! After all, He uses us, and far too often, we're sure no picnic in the park.

Use God's Word to Keep Perspective on God Himself

A radio caller told us about a childhood experience in her parents' church. They were heavily involved in the church's ministry, attending whenever the doors opened, and the minister was quite a strong, forceful man. One night, she said, the minister in mid-service tried his level best to get her to come forward. He informed her she was being called, and if she didn't come forward right that second, she would go to hell. The message and the force with which it was delivered did not send her to the altar; it freaked her out. "I'm healed now to a certain point," she concluded, "but my hair still stands up on the back of my neck whenever I step into a church."

The immediate issue on the table that day was forgiveness. We pointed out that however well the man might have meant, he hurt her. From her perspective, whether he intended to hurt her or save her, he caused damage, and forgiveness for that was in order.

The person who has committed Scripture to memory sees many examples of how the Lord actually dealt with people around Him. Just off the top of my head I can name the woman at the well, the woman taken in adultery, the paralytics, and the demoniacs. It seems Jesus lost patience only with fig trees and spiritually blind Pharisees. Patience, love, and mercy. We asked the young woman to keep in mind that Christ would not have dealt with her the way that minister talked. We have a loving God who is sometimes misrepresented by flawed humans. That is no reflection on God, and actually, not all that much on the humans. But a strong basis of memorized Scripture helps immensely in coming to terms with those flawed humans.

Another caller said he became almost nauseous when he walked into a church, due to a bad childhood experience. His memory was due for a reality check. Rick Fowler provided an excellent illustration for that. His son, then age ten, loved spaghetti. One day he got stomach flu, not long after eating spaghetti for dinner. He lost it. He still doesn't eat spaghetti. "Maybe in a few more years," he says. It wasn't the spaghetti that caused the illness, of course, it was a virus. The spaghetti just got caught in the cross fire.

Similarly, a virus of negatives can affect anyone's spiritual dimension. Missionary kids say, "Mom and Dad were always so busy they never had time for me. I'll never be a missionary!" (Sometimes, unfortunately, they say they'll never be a Christian.) I've heard that statement more times than I care to think about. In these and in many other ways, so many people struggle with bad memories that make God a painful entity. The virus causes the damage, not the spaghetti. The spaghetti gets the blame.

The antidote? The nature of God, committed to memory! Here is the spiritual dimension of what we have been working on all along. We blunt and block the bad memories with good ones. We train the mind by exercising the body.

"I had the opposite experience," claims Brian Newman. "The minister of music in our church when I was growing up sort of took me under his wing. I have many fond memories of that mentoring relationship. He helped me grow in God and love God."

Brian comes forth with another suggestion I want to mention here. "When you think about someone who has influenced your life in such a positive way, jot them a note and say, 'Hey, I appreciate you, and I appreciate the positive effect you had on my life.' "

I read somewhere that 20 percent of life is negative to start with. Good memories need at least as much attention as the negative ones get.

We are not supposed to keep all this to ourselves. We're also instructed to teach the children. And not by preaching, either.

God Tells Us to Teach the Children

"I took my Rachel, about four, out for ice cream one evening, only the two of us," Brian said. "I decided to take Debi's car instead of mine, just in case ice cream got on the seat, you know? Then the remorse set in. What memory was that going to give her? So, while we were waiting for our ice cream, I apologized. I told Rachel that I was wrong to think like that. People are always more important than things. 'Sometimes Dad forgets that,' I said. 'You remind him, okay?' When we came home, the first thing she said was, 'Mom, I learned from Dad that people are more important than things.'

"The clincher is, two days later, she brought it up in her bedtime prayers."

"When you teach something is when you really learn it," a Red Cross first aid instructor said. He's right. In fact, what we teach our children is to remember. The more kids commit to memory—this is just as true with them as it is with us—the more resources they will have to fall back on when the going gets tough. We teach them to remember the blessings God gives us. When doubts assail them, they'll *know* about God's faithfulness.

It's true when you are modeling God for your children, as Brian and I try to do.

This is another reason my family and I spend time together, out on the ranch, around a campfire, singing songs, telling stories. Repetition, repetition, repetition. More than one avenue of learning. Make it a part of them.

"Brainwashing," says the doubter.

"Building confidence," says Buffalo Frank the storyteller. (I'll give you a hint who that is: every time Buffalo Frank gets going with his stories, my girls all say, "Oh, Daa-dee!") "Kids today need all the solid moral confidence they can get."

And they need it close to their hearts where they can use it.

Precious Memories

Memories to guide the children. Memories to guide us. I hope by now you can appreciate that the most powerful instrument you will ever own or use is that two-fist-sized organ between your ears. I ask God's blessing on you and on it that with it you can find perfect peace and joy and purpose in His will.

> Precious memories, unseen angels,
> Sent from somewhere to my soul.
> How they linger, ever near me,
> And the sacred past unfolds.
>
> Precious father, loving mother,
> Fly across the lonely years.
> And old home scenes of my childhood
> In the stillness of the midnight,
> In fond memory appears
> Echoes from the past I hear.
>
> In the stillness of the midnight,
> Echoes from the past I hear.
> Old time singing, gladness bringing,
> From that lovely land somewhere.

As I travel on life's pathway,
Know not what the years may hold.
As I ponder, hope grows fonder,
Precious memories flood my soul.

Precious memories, how they linger,
How they ever flood my soul.
In the stillness of the midnight,
Precious sacred scenes unfold.

Minirth Meier New Life Clinic Series Resources

The Anger Workbook by Dr. Les Carter and Dr. Frank Minirth.
In this book, Drs. Carter and Minirth offer a unique thirteen-step program that will help you identify the best ways to handle anger, uncover and eliminate the myths that perpetuate anger, and identify patterns of relating, thinking, and behaving that influence your anger.

Don't Let the Jerks Get the Best of You by Dr. Paul Meier.
Dr. Meier combines years of counseling with a light-hearted look at his own life in this handbook on human relationships to help you be aware when you are being manipulated or abused, understand how your past can influence your reactions to people now, identify your own "jerk" tendencies, and develop and nurture mature relationships based on respect.

The Father Book by Dr. Frank Minirth, Dr. Brian Newman, and Dr. Paul Warren.
In this instruction manual for fathers, the authors explore what it means to be a father, how fathering has changed in the nineties, and how fathers can meet many of their children's needs as no one else can.

The Headache Book by Dr. Frank Minirth.
Encyclopedic in scope, yet easy to read, this book defines the different types of headaches—sinus, migraine, tension, cluster, and others—where they come from, and how to prevent and/or manage the pain.

Hope for the Perfectionist by Dr. David Stoop.
If you are a perfectionist, or if you live with one, this is the book for you! Insights and answers for those who struggle with the pain and frustration of being a perfectionist.

Imperative People by Dr. Les Carter.

For "those who must be in control," this book confronts the reader with such questions as: 1) Do your emotions control your actions? 2) Are you driven by duty? 3) Do you act superior, yet feel inferior? 4) Do you have a craving for control? An excellent resource for groups dealing with control addictions, codependency, and church leadership.

Kids Who Carry Our Pain by Dr. Robert Hemfelt and
    Dr. Paul Warren.

How do we break the cycle of codependency? How do we keep from passing our childhood wounds down to our own children? The relationship we had with our own parents influences our relationship with our own children—but we can stop the pain and build strong, healthy, happy family ties. This book points the way with compelling stories and profound insights. An excellent resource for groups on codependency, parenting, divorce and single parent issues, and family intimacy.

The Lies We Believe by Dr. Chris Thurman.

Dr. Thurman uncovers the common lies that make us unhappy and ineffectual in our lives, our careers, our families, and our relationship with God, including:

    Self-lies—"I must have everyone's love and approval."

    Worldly lies—"You can have it all."

    Marital lies—"You should meet all my needs."

    Religious lies—"God's love must be earned."

    An excellent resource for groups on codependency, religious addiction, workaholism, depression, or marriage and family intimacy issues.

Love Hunger by Dr. Frank Minirth, Dr. Paul Meier,
    Dr. Robert Hemfelt, and Dr. Sharon Sneed.

Overeaters crave food to satisfy their hunger for love. People with a food addiction have a codependent relationship with food. Part 1 of the this book explores the emotional causes of compulsive overeating and the addiction cycle, and explains how to feed the hungry heart. Part 2 is a ten-stage life plan for body, mind, and soul—a plan not only for controlling weight but for achieving spiritual and emotional healing. Part 3 is the Love Hunger Cookbook, filled with indexed recipes and workable menu plans to fit any lifestyle, plus a guide to nutrition and calories.

Love Hunger Weight-Loss Workbook by Dr. Frank Minirth,
    Dr. Paul Meier, Dr. Robert Hemfelt, and Dr. Sharon Sneed.

This recovery program, which is proven effective by hundreds of support groups at the Minirth Meier New Life Clinic, is now available in a powerful twelve-week interactive workbook. Powerful, practical, and filled with encouraging stories and memorable graphics. Also contains menus, snack choices, and a list of recommended frozen dinners and main dishes.

Love Is a Choice by Dr. Robert Hemfelt, Dr. Frank Minirth,
    and Dr. Paul Meier.

Probably the definitive book on codependency from a Christian perspective. If you have been trying to "fix" an addicted loved one; if you are exhausted from trying to please other people; if you are plagued by guilt, or if you are trapped in a destructive relationship—this book is for you.

Love Is a Choice Workbook by Dr. Robert Hemfelt,
    Dr. Frank Minirth, Dr. Paul Meier, Dr. Deborah Newman,
    and Dr. Brian Newman.

This interactive workbook takes the life-changing principles of *Love Is a Choice* a step further. More than just questions and answers, this workbook is lively reading, packed with stories and graphics that bring the truths and insights of *Love Is a Choice* alive.

Passages of Marriage by Dr. Frank and Mary Alice Minirth, Dr. Brian and Dr. Deborah Newman, and Dr. Robert and Susan Hemfelt.

Marriages go through certain well-defined stages (or "passages") of emotional and spiritual development. This book examines the passages from "Young Love" to "Realistic Love" to "Comfortable Love" to "Renewing Love" to "Transcendent Love," and shows couples how to negotiate successfully the twists and turns of each stage. A beneficial resource for groups on couples support and family intimacy.

The Thin Disguise: Understanding and Overcoming Anorexia and Bulimia by Pam Vredevelt, Dr. Deborah Newman, Harry Beverly, and Dr. Frank Minirth.

The most complete, authoritative book on how to understand and overcome anorexia and bulimia in women, combining sound medical knowledge, psychological principles, and the spiritual principles necessary for recovery. Authors include the nutritional information necessary to reprogram the anorexic's and bulimic's eating habits and advise them how to change their eating habits to regain healthy nutrition.

Things That Go Bump in the Night by Dr. Paul Warren and Dr. Frank Minirth.

The doctors of the Minirth Meier New Life Clinic help parents understand the fears that come with each stage of a child's development. They show how parents can partner with the child to combat and resolve the natural fears of childhood.

The Truths We Must Believe by Dr. Chris Thurman.

The key to emotional health is knowing the truth, facing the truth, and living by the truth. The truths we must believe include:

You don't have to please everyone.

You are going to die.

You are not entitled.

Your childhood isn't over.

A valuable resource for men's and women's groups, emotional health support groups, codependency groups, or any setting where people want to live a full, well-adjusted Christian life.

These and other fine books from Thomas Nelson Publishers are available at a bookstore near you.